I0455370

Blacks and Poverty

Black People's Failure to Embrace and Benefit from the Technological Revolution and a Suggestion for Changing the Tide

Raymond L. Chukwu

authorHOUSE®

AuthorHouse™
1663 Liberty Drive
Bloomington, IN 47403
www.authorhouse.com
Phone: 1 (800) 839-8640

© 2016 Raymond L Chukwu. All rights reserved.

No part of this book may be reproduced, stored in a retrieval system, or transmitted by any means without the written permission of the author.

Published by AuthorHouse   04/07/2016

ISBN: 978-1-5246-0265-9 (sc)
ISBN: 978-1-5246-0266-6 (hc)
ISBN: 978-1-5246-0264-2 (e)

Library of Congress Control Number: 2016905771

Print information available on the last page.

Any people depicted in stock imagery provided by Thinkstock are models, and such images are being used for illustrative purposes only.
Certain stock imagery © Thinkstock.

This book is printed on acid-free paper.

Because of the dynamic nature of the Internet, any web addresses or links contained in this book may have changed since publication and may no longer be valid. The views expressed in this work are solely those of the author and do not necessarily reflect the views of the publisher, and the publisher hereby disclaims any responsibility for them.

Contents

To my best friend, Tennyson O. Chukwu, known to his pals as TOC, who passed away in Lagos, Nigeria, on December 23, 2011, eight years after he visited the United States for the first time. He was a champion for education and spent his life advocating for academic advances in science and technology. He believed this was the only way black people could achieve economic equality and that a team effort was required to ensure that happened.

At the age of fifteen he had experienced a major tragedy when his father passed away. As the firstborn, TOC worked with his mother to raise his younger brothers and sisters. He knew the importance of an education, and he signed up for little pay as a houseboy to Mazi E. O. Onyubuchi, who was the master of class warfare in the community, so he could pay the fees at a local business school.

He graduated with honors and the ability to type 120 to 200 words a minute, which earned him major recognition and marked a major turning point in his young life. Eventually, he became managing director of the Nigeria National Shipping Line. He stressed that people are poor not because of God but because they refuse to challenge the poverty in their lives. He strongly believed that education is a powerful weapon against poverty. He created the opportunity that allowed me to write this book. I am very proud to say that TOC contributed significantly to my academic and financial success.

Tennyson O. Chukwu

I also dedicate this book to my grandmother, Nnn-Ihe Nwaigbo, whose loving care encouraged me to accomplish many things in my life.

Madam Nnn-Ihe Nwaigbo

Finally, I dedicate this book to my foster parents, Dr. William Koster and the late Mrs. Marcia K. Koster. Without their help, I would not have been able to study aerospace engineering in the United States.

Dr. and Mrs. William Koster

Now that a black man has attained the highest elected office in the country, will the economic problems facing the black community finally be solved? You know the answer!

Foreword

Blacks and Poverty, Raymond L. Chukwu's analysis of the black community's failure to embrace and benefit from the technological revolution, is the first book to seriously analyze this topic and offer suggestions for change. One reason black people are mired in poverty is because they have not harnessed the promise of economic stability offered by the fields of science, technology, and medicine. Chukwu made this argument in his earlier book, *Blacks and Technology: The Shift of Economic Power to Blacks in the 21ˢᵗ Century* (2008). In that book, he argued convincingly that blacks do not have any influence in the science, medical, or technology arenas because they have limited access to those fields. This imbalance is exacerbated because African Americans, Chukwu contended, prefer to pursue careers in athletics or entertainment instead of seeking education in mathematics, engineering, or computer technology. Furthermore, when they do achieve success, they do not reinvest their money in organizations that promote and support science, technology, and medicine in black communities. Chukwu believes that only by embracing those fields will black people finally shed the shackles of their oppressors and colonizers and take full advantage of Sub-Saharan natural resources, which will ensure superior economic security. Only through such efforts, he argues, can black people develop the technologies and products—including medicine derived from Sub-Saharan herbs—to treat the diseases that affect their community.

During the entire history of civilized medicine, black people have been diagnosed with instruments, tools, and tests developed through research that excluded the black population. Chukwu suggests that black people should be very skeptical about the statistics that have emerged from such research—for example, the purported incidence of high blood pressure in black men. He concludes that "no accurate medical diagnoses currently exist in the medical literature to convincingly prove otherwise." This complete isolation of the black population from the early medical research reverberates today in the poor relationship between doctors and black patients, who believe they do not get adequate treatment. Chukwu strongly believes that blacks can lift themselves out of poverty by pursuing careers in the fields of science, technology, and medicine.

Blacks and Poverty presents historical facts that explain why black people—in the United States and around the world—are more likely to have limited access to the opportunities afforded by technology and adequate health care. Chukwu—who has been a Republican candidate for the US Congress, a nominee for the post of US ambassador to Nigeria, an aerospace engineer, and president of Black Technologies Advancement—delivers hard-hitting evidence of poor health care in the black community, dating back to colonialism. He explains

- ✓ why black people today continue to experience inadequate medical services;
- ✓ why false presumptions continue to connect serious diseases with black people more than any other group;
- ✓ why leading white medical researchers ignore the benefits offered by Africa's traditional healing remedies, although such treatments are effective in combating many diseases;
- ✓ why black people face higher rates of illnesses, and the actions that can be taken to reverse this trend;
- ✓ the relationship between Africa and major drug corporations, which continue to exploit Africa's resources for their own economic benefit;
- ✓ the economic readiness of black people in the twenty-first century;
- ✓ early scientific and technological discoveries by black people;
- ✓ the real reason black people have been unable to identify the causes of their economic problems;
- ✓ solutions for changing the status quo; and
- ✓ how the black community can overcome poverty and gain economic power in the twenty-first century.

Chukwu also examines Africa's historical role in providing other countries with medical remedies—through extracts from plants and other sources still in use today. He should be applauded: because black people were excluded from early medical research trials, no one has previously provided an accurate medical history of the black community. Modern medical procedures and technologies are all based on the early research from which black people were excluded.

This book comes at the right time, because until this point, no one has challenged the accuracy of the medical deficiencies attributed to black people, especially here in the United States. Rather than questioning or challenging the reliability of these hypotheses, black people accept them without objection. There should be high level of interest in books that address issues of this nature. Everyone, regardless of ethnicity, should be anxious to find out the reasons for the medical challenges faced by black people all over the world. At this point, it is very difficult, if not impossible, for any physician—regardless of qualifications or experience—to diagnose his or her black patients and accurately prescribe the most appropriate medication or treatment.

I strongly believe that this is a very important book. I do not know of anyone else who is so concerned about the quality of life in the black community and so eager to do something about it. That, in itself, is very refreshing.

Carine Tanga

Preface

Blacks and Poverty was written in the period following the 2008 election of Barack Obama as the forty-fourth and first black president of the United States. It takes the form of an exciting discussion on the following topic: Can the election of President Obama encourage black people to challenge the status quo and embrace the science, technological, and medical fields that are so tied to economic success? Science, technology, and medicine offer opportunities that will allow the black community to be a major economic power in the twenty-first century.

I believe that poverty rules the African American community because it has never embraced science and technology education; instead, it has identified with athletes and entertainers. This book explains why black people have failed to welcome the technological revolution.

In the precolonial period, black people enjoyed good health and superior medical care—traditional remedies and medicines made from natural resources. These systems of medicine can by no means be considered empirical. They were based on a considerable amount of knowledge accumulated, by and large, through the application of scientific methods; individual observations and confirmation of those observations by others; formulation of hypotheses; and the testing of the hypotheses via experimentation. Granted, some of the tools used were primitive, but the approach was undoubtedly scientific. Accordingly, Africans developed remarkable drugs to treat various diseases from herbs and other plants long before colonization.

In other words, for centuries, Africans were well equipped to confront medical problems. There were miraculous successes in the control and treatment of many diseases in Sub-Saharan Africa. These successes contributed significantly to the continued popularity of plant-based remedies among Africans, in part because of their ready availability. But colonial officials sought to seriously disrupt the dynamics of plant-based traditional medicine in the areas under their control. Considering the effectiveness of these remedies, there was absolutely no way Sub-Saharan Africans would give them up without a serious fight.

I cannot overemphasize how urgent it is that black people engage in science-, technology-, or medical-related careers. As I explain below, Africa's limited access to technology is the root cause for the fall of black civilization and the current economic status of black people all over the world today. Before colonization, the African's most sophisticated weapons were bows and arrows, which were sufficient for hunting purposes. Realizing that Africa offered abundant resources—people, minerals, crops, land—colonizers utilized superior weapons to launch an all-out assault on the African continent. This marked the beginning of the fall of black civilization and the rise of white civilization in Sub-Saharan Africa.

As you will see in this book, the fall of black people and the rise of white people is the principal reason Sub-Saharan Africans were excluded from the early scientific research on which every medical tool and pharmaceutical are based. This book aims to answer the question: *is technology against black people, or are black people against technology?*

In the 1960s, two prominent black leaders emerged to end this type of exclusion. Dr. Nnamdi Azikiwe was an American-educated, Nigerian political scientist. According to his autobiography, he met secretly with Dr. Martin Luther King Jr. during his education in the United States. The two men discussed the negative influence of the white oppression on black nations. After Azikiwe completed his education in 1959, he returned to Nigeria, teamed up with Kwame Nkrumah of Ghana, and began to execute the strategies he'd discussed with King. Due to the successful execution of those strategies Azikiwe became the first president of Nigeria in 1960 when the country gained its independence from Britain.

King was inspired by the progress in Nigeria and began a similar movement in the United States around 1963–64. These efforts were partly successful, because racial and social justice were achieved, but economic oppression has continued, partially because of black people's limited involvement in science, medicine, and technology.

Given Azikiwe's major contributions in this area, it is very troubling that his name remains obscure in history of the black struggle. I certainly have no explanation for that. The important thing to note is that black people were successful because they were united as a team and fought for a defined purpose—probably for the first time in black history. Otherwise, no black leader has emerged to perform at the same level. The achievements of blacks since then has been on an individual basis, which has not addressed this problem. The election of Barack Obama did not address the failure of black people to embrace the technological revolution as the prerequisite for enjoying the following benefits offered by a robust economy:

- ✓ economic power
- ✓ superior defense capabilities
- ✓ domestic and international prestige
- ✓ superior business creditability
- ✓ advanced academic achievements in science, technology, and medicine

It is surprising that Obama has never called for a black economic summit with entertainers and scientists (e.g., engineers) and then tried to build strong business relationships between both groups. In these early years of the twenty-first century, black people could have generated the necessary momentum to unite in the fight against poverty, using the natural resources of Sub-Saharan Africa.

Acknowledgments

I thank the following people, who have contributed extensively to my success:

The late Tennyson O. Chukwu (Nigeria)
Reverend Duggon (France)
Reverend Scott Campbell (France)
Dr. William Koster (United States)
The late Mrs. Marcia Koster (United States)
Joe King (France)
Joe Sow (Senegal)
Augustine Asiakw (France)
Francis Ironkwe (Senegal)
Mazi Nwaeyi (Cameroon)
The late Darlington Chukwu (Nigeria)
Uche Okoro (Nigeria)

Finally, I give special thanks to all whose support, encouragement, and motivation influenced my decision to write this book.

"The Struggling Boy from Sub-Saharan Africa"

Raymond L. Chukwu

My God, my God.
Of all the races you created,
the black race is the coolest one,
because of its abundant natural resources.
My God, my God,
Of all the races I know,
the black race worships you the most.
Yet blacks face the worst poverty.
Why, why, my God, my God?
My God, my God.
Of all the continents I know,
the wealthiest is black Africa,
because of its natural resources.
My God, my God.
Given these blessings and worship history,
why, why, why, my God,
does the black race suffer the worst poverty?
My God, my God, my God.
Why, why, why, why?

Introduction

Does technology discriminate against black people, or do black people discriminate against technology? Regardless of the answer, black people must identify with science, technology, and medicine before they can achieve sustained economic security. Poverty in the black community can be attributed to the fact that blacks as a race are not associated with these fields, which are required for economic security.

Before we develop a solution to any kind of a problem, we must identify the cause of the problem. Over the decades, black people, including their leaders, have fought for equality but have failed to achieve economic equality, because they have not identified the cause of their economic problems.

The abundant natural resources of Sub-Saharan Africa make that region an important participant in the twenty-first-century global economy. Given the rapid depletion of the resources in the rest of the world, Sub-Saharan African nations are expected to dominate the world economy in the not too distant future.

This book is called *Blacks and Poverty*. It analyzes black people's failure to embrace and benefit from the technological revolution and offers a solution for changing the tide. This is because, despite decades of effort, Sub-Saharan Africa is poorer today than it was in 1960, in some cases by very wide margins. These African nations have been the sites of large-scale experiments to reform their economies, and yet their people are malnourished or starving. However, these ambitious projects have failed to generate sustained economic growth.

Nigeria, for example, has abundant natural resources, including crude oil, and a highly skilled labor force and is considered the most prosperous segment in the world economy. There are more than ten million Nigerians with college degrees in the United States, Europe, Asia, Australia, and South Africa. They are in self-imposed exile, because the Nigerian economy cannot accommodate their academic achievements. This self-imposed exile frustrates Nigerians, as more than 90 percent of them hold jobs that pay 50 percent below the amount generally paid to someone with those degrees. Why should more than 137 million Nigerians—as well as citizens of other Sub-Saharan African nations—be subject to this type of economic torture? The sheer magnitude of this problem calls for an urgent and innovative approach to reform the social and economy climate in Sub-Saharan Africa.

Even though black people have made progress over the years, they still need to achieve economic power, domestic and international prestige, a superior business reputation, and academic degrees in science, technology, and medicine. Such achievements will ensure that they enjoy the same economic opportunities as their counterparts of Asian and European heritage living in the United States and other parts of the world.

Food security exists when everyone has access to sufficient amounts of safe, nutritious and affordable food to provide the foundation for an active and healthy life. Given that food security affects human health and welfare as well as economic and political stability, we must increase food security in Sub-Saharan African nations. Malnourishment, population growth, agricultural production, and changing consumption trends pose significant challenges to Sub-Sahara Africa.

Growing populations and reduced per capita income will add to the demand for food in the region. As I will describe in this book, technology is one way to overcome major obstacles to food security, such as supply disruptions, government policies that inhibit trade and negatively affect farmers, growth of biofuels, environmental impact, declining R&D investment, and price volatility. Food security can be assured by honoring comparative advantage, enabling open markets, supporting small farmers, fostering cooperation between the public and private sectors, encouraging agricultural investment, and reforming biofuels mandates.

Africa's agricultural performance has been insufficient given its high population growth; this has led to a decline in per capita production.

Development and utilization of nanotechnology, through molecular manipulations, is expected to provide opportunities in food and water safety that could have a significant impact on rural populations in Sub-Saharan Africa. Technology is cost and energy efficient and safety compliant. It is important to recognize that the results from research and demonstrations may contribute significantly to the development of future technologies for African nations, which will benefit local farmers.

Even though progress has been made by black people over the years, they still must achieve economic power, domestic and international prestige, a superior business reputation, and advanced academic degrees in science, technology, and medicine before they can enjoy the same economic opportunities as their counterparts of Asian and European heritage living in the United States and other parts of the world.

Asian Americans and European Americans control the economic power of the United States, and the world, because of their interest in the research and development of science, technology, and medicine. Because of this commitment, these ethnic groups are now identified with an incredible technology base—here in the United States and in their home countries. However, the poverty in the black community has increased over the years.

Chapter 1

Current Economic Status of Black People

The basic problem confronting black people and their leaders in this country today is the inability to determine the root cause of their economic problems and develop realistic plans for addressing those problems. Black people neither have any market share nor hold any influence in the science, technology, or medical arenas. This is a disturbing trend that demands an honest inquiry. The right answer will be, "Black people do not have any market share or any influence in the world, because they have no products to offer. The market is a two-way street; you buy my product, and I buy yours. It is as simple as that."

After readers review the data in this book, they will realize that black people still have a long way to go in their efforts to wield influence in the medical, technological, and scientific fields. In my opinion, this is not only disappointing but troubling. Black people, including black leaders, do not understand that without science, technology, or medical backgrounds, they will never be a productive part of the medical or scientific communities or participate and enjoy the current economic boom in the United States. Unfortunately, the election of Barack Obama, the first black man to hold the office of the president of the United States, has not done anything to change this equation. If Obama had organized a community-development summit with black entertainers and scientists, what an exciting discussion could have taken place. If people in those fields worked together to establish a high-tech corporation designed to embrace opportunity, the entire black community would benefit. It would change the tide for black people at this moment.

Black leaders emphasize that it is imperative to build philosophical bridges from Wall Street to Appalachia and the Delta, and from prosperous Silicon Valley to the ghettos, barrios, and lonesome hillsides in the Ozarks and Middle America. They say these bridges will be built if we focus on the following:

- ✓ access to capital
- ✓ quality education for all children
- ✓ the prison-industrial complex
- ✓ human rights around the world
- ✓ comprehensive health care for all Americans
- ✓ coalition building and shared economic interest

The only thing in this list that relates to economic struggle is the lack of a quality education. Yet no one explains that, at this time, education alone is not sufficient to obtain any market share in the marketplace. Black people must seek degrees in the fields of science, medicine, engineering, mathematics, and computer technology. Only then will they operate at the same level as other ethnic groups. If blacks have no products to sell, they will continue to buy from others, which means that no one will buy anything from them. It is difficult, if not impossible, to get access to capital without a market base or to form profitable trading partnerships. To have a measurable impact in the marketplace, a product must demonstrate scientific merit and technological feasibility. Given the limited participation of blacks in science or technology, they will struggle to benefit from the development of such products and will have no share in the world economy.

This leads me to the question: does technology discriminate against black people, or do black people discriminate against technology? Regardless of the answer, black people must be recognized as contributing members of the scientific or technology industries before they can gain any market share. Can black people achieve superior economic status in the twenty-first century after they have been suppressed and oppressed for more than one hundred years? Before the slave trade and the colonization of Sub-Saharan Africa, black Africans had prestige, integrity, and economic power. The slave trade and the colonization brought an end to that. As we begin the twenty-first century, black people's efforts to regain their integrity, prestige, and superior economic status has been disrupted by their limited access to the scientific, technological, and medical fields.

Before colonization, black Africans had untapped natural resources, most of which are still untapped. This is due in part to limited

2

scientific and technological knowledge—the prerequisites for economic security. Black people have not been exposed to the education and training they need to gain such skills. Table 1997 1a shows the percentage of the US black population involved in the engineering, science, and medical professions. According to this table, the population of this country is about 267 million; white people comprise 82 percent (220 million), and black people comprise 13 percent (34 million) people. There are approximately 1.67 million engineers in the United States; 1.48 million (88 percent) are white, and only 58,000 (3 percent) are black. Of the 409,000 scientists in the United States, 358,000 (88 percent) are white, and only 17,000 (4 percent) are black. Of the 875,000 doctors in the United States, 759,000 (87 percent) are white, and only 28,000 (3 percent) are black.

	General population	**White**	**Black**	**White %**	**Black%**
Population	267 Million	220 Million	34 Million	82%	13%
Engineers	1.7 Million	1.5 Million	58,000	88%	3%
Scientists	409,000	358,000	17,000	88%	4%
Doctors	875,000	759,000	28,000	87%	3%

Table 1a: Analysis of the occupations held by white and black people. Compiled from the Housing and Household Economic Statistics Division, US Department of Commerce.

These data illustrate the state of the black community today in the United States. They illustrate the impact limited access to education and opportunity have on economic success. These figures should be offensive to black people; they are a call for collective action to change these humiliating statistics and historical trends.

An analysis of the relationship between blacks, drugs, and gangs supports the data in table 1. People deprived of opportunities in science and technology might consider drugs and gangs as an alternative pathway to economic power. Table 1b lists the racial breakdown of the US prison population. Of the 1.6 million people in prison, 31 percent are black, which is very troubling. Imagine how many people could be turned away from gangs if there were more opportunities for careers in science, technology, and medicine.

	General	White	Black	White %	Black %
Population	267 million	220 million	34 million	82%	13%
Imprisoned	1.6 million	464,000	502,000	28%	31%

Table 1b: Racial breakdown of the US prison population.

To correct this unpleasant situation once and for all, we first must identify the principal cause of this problem. Unless we deal with the situation represented by the data in table 1, it is difficult to imagine that we can resolve the complex challenges facing the black community.

Sports
Black people play pivotal roles in professional sports in the United States but they have been unable to employ this success to improve their economic status. This too is associated with the data in table 1a. Let me explain.

Today, many black athletes are the fastest runners in the world, yet they lack the mathematical knowledge to accurately calculate their speed. In many ways, it is much more difficult to do the dash than to do the math. Here is an example to illustrate my point: the air we breathe is composed of nitrogen, oxygen, carbon dioxide, and other atmospheric particles. Because these atmospheric particles are constantly in motion, they create opposing resistance to movement. Now, to win at the hundred-meter dash, a sprinter has to overcome strong air resistance in record time, carry and propel his own weight, and maintain total control of various external and internal conditions. To be successful, the sprinter must develop a wide range of skills, abilities, and habits:

- ✓ vigorous training
- ✓ concentration
- ✓ focus
- ✓ self-confidence

✓ determination
✓ courage
✓ willpower
✓ self-discipline
✓ body dynamics (or the maneuverability to overcome the air resistance in record time)

However, too many black students have been told that it is more difficult to calculate the velocity and the acceleration of the sprinter than to do the sprint itself. In other words, the skills needed to *do the math* are twice the skills needed to *do the dash*. If one needed only half of the wisdom, painstaking effort, willpower, and self-discipline it takes to become a sprinter to become either an engineer or scientist, we probably would not have any engineers or scientists in the world today. In spite of this, black people go through life feeling inferior when they should be feeling superior; they have superior talents and intelligence, but they don't have enough opportunities to put these abilities to the test.

Let's examine the following sports, which in the United States are dominated by black athletes.

Football
Football is the most competitive sport in the United States, and it is dominated almost entirely by black players. On most teams, 88 percent of the players are black. To play in this competitive sport, an athlete must have the following:

✓ endurance
✓ ability to outsmart an opponent
✓ ability to train extensively
✓ determination and willpower
✓ solid and strong self-confidence
✓ body dynamics—that is, the ability to overcome the massive collisions associated with the game while maintaining total control of one's external and internal conditions

Again, it takes a lot more to become a football player than it does to become an engineer or scientist, but black people have been told otherwise.

Basketball

This is another competitive sport in the United States that is also dominated almost entirely by black players. As was the case with football, each basketball team has more than 88 percent of black players. This sport requires the same skills as football:

- ✓ endurance
- ✓ ability to outsmart an opponent
- ✓ ability to train vigorously
- ✓ self-discipline
- ✓ determination
- ✓ self-confidence
- ✓ body dynamics—that is, the ability to overcome the massive collisions associated with the game while maintaining total control of one's external and internal conditions

It takes a lot more to become a basketball player than it does to become an engineer or scientist, but black people have been told otherwise.

Baseball

Baseball is called the all-American sport. It is a very competitive sport in the United States and is dominated almost entirely by black players as well. Each team has more than 70 percent of black players. This sport requires the following skills:

- ✓ endurance
- ✓ ability to outsmart an opponent
- ✓ ability to train extensively
- ✓ determination
- ✓ self-confidence
- ✓ body dynamics—that is, the ability to pitch the ball in the most skillful manner and the concentration needed to hit the ball forcefully

It takes a lot more effort to become a baseball player than it does to become an engineer or scientist, but black people have accepted fiction rather than fact.

Boxing

This is another intriguing sport that is mostly dominated by black people in the United States. Boxing is a one-on-one sport. It requires agility and physical fitness. It also requires the ability to throw and take heavy punches. Boxing is almost entirely dominated by black fighters. More than 90 percent of the boxers in the United States are black. An excellent boxer must exhibit the following skills:

- ✓ agility
- ✓ endurance
- ✓ ability to outsmart an opponent
- ✓ ability to train vigorously
- ✓ self-discipline
- ✓ determination
- ✓ self-confidence
- ✓ body dynamics (ability to outsmart and confuse your opponent)

	White %	Black %
Track	20	80
Football	12	88
Basketball	11	89
Baseball	30	70
Boxing	10	90

Table 1c: Statistical breakdown of the racial composition of American sport teams

If you compare tables 1a and 1c, you will notice an amazing similarity between the percentages for white and black. Representing only 13 percent of the population, black people dominate the field events, with an 83.4 percent average. This is a commendable and outstanding record. Yet, no significant progress has been made in this area to improve the image, prestige, or economic status of black people. It is sad that few professional sports teams are black owned. White people, on other hand, representing 82 percent of the population, dominate science and technology with about 88 percent of the engineers, 88 percent of the scientists, and 87 percent of doctors. This statistical data relates to the superior economic status of white people, who have the know-how to outsmart black people, even in the sports where they dominate.

You do not need to be a rocket scientist to determine, based on tables 1a and 1c, that technology, science, and medicine hold the master key to world power, superior economic status, international prestige, and improved academic status. Can black people ever restore the prestige and integrity they lost during colonization and slave trade? The answer to this question is yes.

If it is true that every adversity carries the seed of equivalent benefit and if that adversity is accepted as a challenge to try harder, then more than one hundred years of devastating struggle and suffering among black people definitely will be rewarded in the early twenty-first century, but only if they accept the challenge to try harder. How this will be successfully accomplished is a complex question. There are many answers, but the correct one is the theme of this book, which provides step-by-step strategies for how black people can shift the economic power toward themselves. It includes methodologies and implementation techniques. It is the first book to tackle the economic status of black people from perspective of science, technology, and medicine.

To do this successfully, we must identify the cause of the economic problems in the black community. Table 1a shows that science, technology, and medicine are prerequisites for economic security. Until black people are identified with careers in science, technology, and medicine, their economic problems will continue.

Chapter 2

The Connections between Technology and Poverty in the Black Community

In my opinion, poverty in the black community can be attributed to the fact that black people as a race neither have a technology base nor are associated or involved with any scientific or technological developments. As a result, black people cannot enjoy any of the following benefits:

- ✓ economic power
- ✓ superior defense capabilities
- ✓ domestic and international prestige
- ✓ superior business reputation
- ✓ advanced academic degrees in science, technology, and medicine

The black race is unlike other races, who enjoy all of the benefits listed above because they have technology bases here in the United States. They share these benefits with their home countries, thereby commanding superior economic power in the global economy.

Why are black people where they are today? Several answers might come to mind, but the correct answer is that they are not identified with any science- or technology-related products. A second question might be, why aren't black people identified with science or technology? The two questions have the same answer: every race in this world, including the black race, is here for a specific purpose. Furthermore, every race in this world has strong and weak points. The white race, for example, is always very ambitious and has a defined mission. The black race, on the other hand has skills and talents but refuses to apply its God-given talents to advance the economic status of black people all over the world. Instead, black people always think in terms of individual success.

A large percentage of black people lack the patience and diligence necessary for the long-time, high-risk undertakings involved in development or study of science, technology, or medicine. Table 1a can be used to support this argument, because it compares the number of black people associated with science, technology, and medicine to the number associated with entertainment and sports.

An independent study conducted by Black Technologies Advancement revealed that about 0 percent of black-owned hi-tech businesses in Silicon Valley were prime contractors or subcontractors working for the more than five hundred Department of Defense and other federal government contractors and approximately 3,500 subcontractors that operate in Santa Clara County, California. This is due in part to the fact that blacks have never embraced degrees in science, medicine, and technology. In addition, the black community has missed out on economic stability because it identifies with athletes and entertainers at the expense of careers that would have led to success. This book discusses why black community failed to welcome the technological revolution, specifically:

- ✓ why the black community disproportionately suffers from poor health care in the United States and around the world
- ✓ the real reason black community is unable to identify the cause of its economic problems
- ✓ new solutions for changing the status quo
- ✓ how the black community can overcome poverty and gain economic power in the twenty-first-century economy

These factors have contributed to the considerable gap that exists between the skills of staff at white-owned hi-tech companies and those at black-owned hi-tech businesses. This imbalance compromises the ability of black businesses to compete for contracts issued by federal and state governments and private corporations (see table 2a).

While the business world is a constantly changing dynamic system and no longer depends on a large, stable workforce with a limited knowledge base, it is hard for black-owned hi-tech businesses to succeed, because it is difficult for them to hire employees with the necessary skills to increase productivity and maximize profit or to train staff in those skills. Training developed with limited resources has failed to produce the skills needed, because even those with advanced degrees still need practical experience, which certainly requires sophisticated facilities and resources and in most cases exceeds the budgets of black-owned hi-tech businesses.

In an era of scarce resources, rapid change, and fierce global competition, black-owned businesses will need help in order to compete successfully.

Because black-owned businesses do not have adequate financial backing, they lack the sophisticated facilities and resources they need to overcome the high-cost, high-risk, and complex challenges associated with research in science, technology, and medicine. It can take several years of research before the final product goes into the marketplace. This is due to the high risks and high costs associated with such efforts. Black-owned companies lack the necessary resources and capital to undertake such missions. Diverse technical resources are needed. Black-owned businesses experience difficulties as they try to generate funds needed for operations and training. For these businesses to acquire the requisite skills needed to compete and win competitive government contracts, they need government grants or funding.

Unfortunately, laws and regulations make it very difficult, if not impossible, for any black-owned hi-tech businesses to receive the research grants they need to be competitive and to expand their businesses as well (see table 2a).

	White %	Black %	Hispanic %	Asian %
Research grants	90	.4	1.5	8

Table 2a: Distribution of federal government research grants, sorted by type of ownership. Compiled by Black Technologies Advancement.

This makes it very unlikely that black-owned hi-tech businesses will receive enough research grants to fund their operations, and thus provide employment opportunities and make a significant contribution to the economic status of black people.

Without impressive employment experience and evidence of successful product development, black workers and black-owned hi-tech businesses cannot contribute to the black community. If, on the other hand, black-owned hi-tech businesses were able to design products that sold well in the marketplace, they would achieve economic benefits and educate black people on ways for improving the general quality of life. Black-owned businesses and their employees may not get to the top of economic ladder, but their earnings will certainly take them out of poverty and enable them to help other black people as well.

If science, medicine, and technology are to be used to address the economic problems of black people, a first step is to tap African resources and use them to identify the black race with science, technology, and medicine. If, indeed, we are concerned about the black economic progress, we must also understand that any significant progress must originate from Sub-Saharan Africa. Most African natural resources are not a focus of the world market, although they have the potential to generate more than $938 billion a year.

Chapter 3

Science and Technology in Sub-Saharan Africa

Due to the early exclusion of the black population and Sub-Saharan plants from any medical research, the medicinal properties of African plants are not endorsed by the modern medical profession. The biochemical properties of plants growing in Sub-Saharan Africa nations are ignored by the world, and traditional medicines remain obscure, although they have been used as effective treatments for years. This exclusion from scientific and medical research is regrettable. Sub Saharan plants could contribute significantly to drug and economic development in several ways.

Biotechnology-Related Investment Opportunities

- ✓ profitable business relationships
- ✓ use of Sub-Saharan plants in alternative medicines
- ✓ new scientific data to advance medical knowledge
- ✓ identification of black people with science, technology, and medicine

The exclusion of black people and African natural resources from medicine is a catastrophe.

- ✓ Tropical plants are an important source of bioactive natural products.
- ✓ Many chemotherapeutic agents used in modern medicine are derived from plants.
- ✓ The high percentage of promising drugs developed from herbs illustrates the chemical diversity of native African plants.
- ✓ Sub-Sahara Africa's tropical forest ecosystems are threatened by development and modernization as is the botanical knowledge associated with traditional cultural practices.
- ✓ Many of today's pharmaceuticals have their origins in plants.

We need to generate new concepts in order to accelerate the development of new pharmaceuticals from Sub-Saharan plants. Such investigations should proceed with a defined scientific plan that explores the medical merits and market potentials. Given the anticipated market penetration and the commercial potential, there is no reason for black people to be where they are today. This is particularly true regarding to their sad experiences with modern medicine. Drugs are a means for relieving suffering and achieving and maintaining good health. Over the past six decades, the development of new plant-based drugs has been remarkable. Imagine the miraculous successes that would be achieved in the control and treatment of many diseases through the application of Sub-Saharan African plants in modern medicine. Potential advantages may already be known. Moreover, if the plant are abundant and the compounds easily isolated, the costs of drugs may be greatly reduced.

Since modern medicine arrived in Sub-Saharan Africa with colonialism, it was considered an alien system imposed on the people by force. After African countries achieved independence, there was a renewed interest in the traditional systems of healing, because it is a part of national resurgence. African plants—and the remedies that derive from them—cannot be ignored if black people take advantage of their superior pharmaceutical properties.

Chapter 4

Sub-Saharan Resources

The untapped African natural resources might become the largest market in the world in the twenty-first century. The literature of every ancient culture contains accounts of natural resources with enormous commercial potential. Unfortunately for these other cultures, their resources are being produced and consumed at an ever-increasing rate. In not-too-distant future, their supply of resources may be depleted.

The resources in Sub-Saharan Africa have been ignored by major industries, for no reason other than that the West has successfully convinced the world that everything about black people is inferior. However, this ignoring of Sub-Saharan resources might have been the best thing that ever happened Africa, because its resources are ready explode in world market in these early years of the twenty-first century. That certainly will put the black community at a different level, particularly if black people capitalize on this opportunity. One way to do this is to hold a black summit.

Black Summit
The summit would seek to determine whether technology is against black people, or black people are against technology, and determine the reason for black people's economic problems. Without a clear understanding of the problem, it will be difficult, if not impossible, to find a solution. Attendees—who should include black scientists—can discuss why black people have failed to embrace science, technology, and medicine despite the economic benefits those fields offer, including the following:

- ✓ economic power
- ✓ superior defense capabilities
- ✓ domestic and international prestige
- ✓ superior business reputation

- ✓ advanced academic degrees in science, technology, and medicine

In addition, they should address the following questions:

- ✓ Will higher paying jobs allow black people to enjoy these benefits?
- ✓ How will higher paying jobs be created considering that those jobs are dependent on new products entering the marketplace?

Action Plan

During the summit, attendees will review the scenarios listed below to develop a comprehensive action plan:

- ✓ Determine the prerequisites needed to achieve a robust economy.
- ✓ Explain how creating higher paying jobs will address this problem.
- ✓ Identify the types of higher paying jobs best suited for the black community
- ✓ Target technologies and products that can be derived from Sub-Saharan natural resources, particularly minerals.
- ✓ Discuss the potential benefits.
- ✓ Determine how those benefits will allow black people to compete with others.

Invite black scientists to attend the summit to study the potential use of Sub-Saharan minerals in nanotechnology, which involves measuring and manipulating matter at the atomic, molecular, and supra-molecular levels. Attendees will do the following:

- ✓ Explain why developing nanotechnology that uses Sub-Saharan minerals is an appropriate action plan.
- ✓ Target the techniques that are based on the incorporation of nanotechnology.
- ✓ Discuss the benefits of pure carbon fibers associated with Sub-Saharan minerals that exhibit extraordinary electrical, magnetic, optical, mechanical, and other physical properties.

✓ Explain how these physical properties apply to the design of chips and textures in the form of coded expert knowledge as the key intelligence tools.
✓ Discuss how the disruption in our computer systems, bio-terrorism threats, and other intelligence-related failures can be attributed to failures on our artificial intelligence and networking capabilities.
✓ Explain how the applications of these properties for the design of chips and codes that form the basis of intelligent tools that can, for example, deal with threats of terrorism.
✓ Given that no African nations have any defense capabilities, the application of molecular manipulations based upon nanotechnology will give black people the superior defense capabilities and domestic and international prestige that they currently lack.
✓ Explain why advances in nanotechnology present new opportunities that will improve the quality of life.
✓ Discuss how to address the risks associated with nanotechnology.

Implementation Strategies
During the summit, attendees will examine various industries and technologies to determine how black people can establish superior defense capabilities and gaining domestic and international prestige. They will assess if this approach can put black people at the forefront of the requirements for twenty-first-century warfare.

Two key groups will be instrumental in meeting this objective:

✓ investors and entertainers
✓ scientists, technology experts, and doctors

To successfully achieve this objective, both groups will need to build a relationship based on trust and understanding. Summit attendees should promote investment strategies that design, develop, and deliver scientific products based on key computer-intelligent and user-interactive analysis capabilities based on molecular manipulations.

The goal will be to analyze Sub-Saharan soil moisture and the biophysical parameters of the land to find ways to improve the cultivation of crops. Furthermore, given the accumulation of waste and recyclables all over Sub-Saharan Africa, attendees should examine the possibilities of using compost and recyclables to equip the black community with better fertilization and cultivation techniques in order to

- ✓ improve efficiency on waste-collection and waste-management processes,
- ✓ improve access to recycling facilities and centers,
- ✓ develop methods for profitable utilization of compost,
- ✓ use compost to engineer robust soil mechanics, and
- ✓ employ engineered soil mechanics to cultivate healthy crops.

Farmers in rural areas can use engineered robust soil mechanics to grow crops that can reduce diseases that confront a large percentage of the population in Sub-Saharan nations. The most disturbing are chronic conditions such as heart disease, cancer, diabetes, hypertension, chronic obstructive disease, and other serious diseases associated with poverty. These diseases are most common among people with low incomes. But treatment costs can run to several hundred million dollars, which the black community cannot afford.

Furthermore, there is a growing consensus within farming communities that the current methodologies will not maximize the production of healthy food products at a cost that can be afforded by low-income families. This emphasizes the need to focus on science, technology, and medical efforts.

Let us examine the availability of these resources in order to accurately predict their potential economic impact and benefit to black people as they struggle to attain superior economic power in the twenty-first century. Let us begin this complex examination with mineral resources, the backbone of the economies of several African countries.

Mineral Resources

Sub-Saharan Africa is probably one of the wealthiest sources of minerals in the world today. Since petroleum is of great interest to the industrial world, especially the United States, we will first examine African petroleum. The world now realizes that oil is being produced and consumed at an ever-increasing rate; in the not-too-distant future, the world's oil supply might be depleted. There is an urgent need to explore scientific ways of developing alternative energy sources, promote energy conservation, and achieve a healthier environment. However, these activities are at the preliminary stages, and no one can predict the impact they will have on the world's oil market.

Nigeria has oil refineries in many parts of the country and is probably the only country in Sub-Saharan Africa that produces and exports oil. According to research conducted by the Young African Engineer Association (YAEA), promising scientific data exists to predict the presence of high volume of drillable oil in many Sub-Saharan countries, such as Cameroon, Togo, Ghana, Ivory Coast, Liberia, Sierra Leone, Senegal, Kenya, Uganda, and Ethiopia. The study also suggests the presence of marketable minerals in these countries, including the following:

- ✓ coal and gold
- ✓ diamonds and uranium
- ✓ lead and zinc
- ✓ limestone and tin
- ✓ columbite and iron ore
- ✓ marble and stone
- ✓ zircon and petroleum

YAEA consists of American and European trained medical personnel and engineers from the following Sub-Saharan countries: Cameroon, Nigeria, Togo, Ghana, Ivory Coast, Liberia, Sierra Leone, Senegal, Kenya, Uganda, and Ethiopia. These untapped mineral resources are expected to attract numerous investment opportunities and create one of the largest markets in the history of the world. This will give black people living in the twenty-first century a superior economic edge over other races for the first time in modern history.

	Liberia	Ghana	Sierra Leone	Nigeria	Senegal	Togo
Coal	x					
Zinc	x	x	x	x	x	x
Gold	x	x	x	x	x	x
Diamonds	x	x				
Uranium	x	x	x			
Petroleum	x	x				
Limestone	x	x	x	x	x	x
Tin	x	x	x	x	x	x
Columbite	x	x	x	x	x	x
Iron ore	x	x	x	x	x	x
Lead	x	x	x	x	x	x
Marble	x	x	x	x	x	x
Stone	x	x	x	x	x	x
Zircon	x	x	x	x	x	x

Table 4a. Untapped Mineral Resources in Some Sub-Saharan Countries: Part 1.

	Kenya	Uganda	Ethiopia	Cameroon
Coal	x	x	x	x
Zinc	x	x	x	x
Gold	x	x		
Diamonds	x	x		
Uranium	x	x	x	
Copper	x	x		
Petroleum	x	x		
Limestone	x	x	x	x
Tin	x	x	x	x
Columbite	x	x	x	x
Iron ore	x	x	x	x
Lead	x	x	x	x
Marble	x	x	x	x

| Stone | x | x | x | x |
| Zircon | x | x | x | x |

Table 4b. Untapped Mineral Resources in Some Sub-Saharan Countries: Part 2.

Agricultural Resources

Can agriculture offer another solution to the economic challenges facing the black race? From every angle of analysis, Africa is a blessed land. Most African countries have a very favorable climate all year round, which is advantageous to the growth and production of health-beneficial crops. Because of the rapid population growth in the industrial world, the consumption of agricultural resources hit a peak, but now it is on the way down, creating glut in the world's food market. The anticipated food shortage associated with the rapid population increase encourage farmers to grow genetically engineered crops to meet the increasing demand. Some of these crops have created complex health problems among a large percentage of the population. Hence, there is an urgent need to produce and supply food products with no artificial ingredients. This will be difficult for many countries, unless they have outside assistance.

African agricultural resources can play a pivotal role in creating a sustainable and dependable global food market. YAEA's research has revealed that the following African agricultural products exhibit superior nutritional characteristics:

- ✓ fruit and nuts
- ✓ bananas and plantains
- ✓ various types of vegetables
- ✓ rice and yams
- ✓ cassava and meat
- ✓ seafood and palm oil

	Liberia	Ghana	Sierra Leone	Nigeria	Senegal	Togo
Fruit	x	x	x	x	x	x
Nuts	x	x	x	x	x	x
Bananas	x	x	x	x	x	x
Plantains	x	x	x	x	x	x
Vegetables	x	x	x	x	x	x
Rice	x	x	x	x	x	x
Yams	x	x	x	x	x	x
Cassava	x	x	x	x	x	x
Meat	x	x	x	x	x	x
Seafood	x	x	x	x	x	x
Palm oil	x	x	x	x	x	x

Table 4c. Superior-quality nutritional agricultural products grown in West Africa.

	Kenya	Uganda	Ethiopia	Cameroon
Fruits	x	x	x	x
Nuts	x	x	x	x
Bananas	x	x	x	x
Plantains	x	x	x	x
Vegetables	x	x	x	x
Rice	x	x	x	x
Yams	x	x	x	x
Cassava	x	x	x	x
Meat	x	x	x	x
Seafood	x	x	x	x
Palm oil	x	x	x	x

Table 4d. Superior-quality nutritional agricultural products grown in Kenya, Uganda, Ethiopia, and Cameroon.

African Plants
Tropical plants are possible sources of drugs to treat malaria; parasitic diseases; diarrhea; infectious diseases, including AIDS;

cardiovascular diseases; respiratory diseases; hepatitis; mental disorders; and other serious illnesses. As a result, biochemical researchers and pharmaceutical companies have been screening and analyzing tropical plants for anti-tumor and AIDS-antiviral medications, and they have tested more than 114,000 extracts from over 35,000 plants. Interestingly, more than 75 percent of these plants come from black Africa. In spite of this high percentage, a large number of African herbs have not been widely utilized in either biomedical research or the biotechnology market, creating additional economic frustration for the black race.

According to the traditional African herbalists, the universe is composed of opposing but interdependent forces. This philosophy resembles the concept of homeostasis, the natural balance that occurs within living organisms, including the harmony between antagonists and agonists that regulate vital functions. Thus, an important factor in the search for new medicine is developing compounds that work together with the body's own restorative and regenerative abilities. To lead healthy lives, we must seek balance with nature, with society, and within ourselves. Through the medicinal and scientific utilization of African herbs, the black race can make a significant contribution to humanity. Unfortunately, however, African herbs are unknown in much of the world communities because of the following:

✓ lack of documented scientific proof
✓ lack of education among African herbalists, who are often senior citizens
✓ lack of knowledge in pharmaceutical science, radiation physics, and nuclear technology
✓ lack of adequate communication with outside world
✓ prevalent poverty
✓ lack of modern technology and resources

No scientific investigation has ever explored African herbs as cost-effective alternative medicines against AIDS, cancer, and other serious illnesses. African herbs could become a biotechnology cornerstone that provides the United States and Africa with several important scientific and economic benefits, including the following:

✓ biotechnology-related investment opportunities
✓ profitable business relationships
✓ wide utilization of Africa herbs as effective alternative medicines

The plants that are the most promising for drug development, including tropical herbs, often are found in ecosystems that are seriously threatened. The terrible irony is that as advances in biology expand our ability to develop new drugs, the raw materials we need to do so are becoming extinct. Also threatened is the traditional knowledge, developed over generations, to identify plants and animals with medicinal value. Social, economic, and political factors—which play a role in employment, poverty, and the lack of economic and educational opportunities—are the underlying causes of this biodiversity crisis.

Efforts to protect biological diversity in Africa will succeed they are if implemented with the involvement of Africans and the understanding that black people's economic prosperity must originate from Sub-Saharan Africa, if the continent can be expected to make any significant contributions and have a lasting economic impact. Research conducted by BTA confirms that African herbs contain a host of potentially useful compounds from which more than 75 percent of biologically effective drugs have been isolated.

If these findings about African herbs are indeed true, the associated scientific merits and technical feasibilities will be very enormous, with virtually unlimited payoffs that will endear their proponents to humankind forever. Testing is required to generate the scientific data needed to advance the pharmacological value of African herbs and identify black people for the first time with medical products.

Effectiveness of African Herbs
Four types of African herbs have remarkable healing characteristics; their backgrounds, histories, and treatment capabilities are discussed briefly below. These three herbs are currently being studied at BTA; to find out more, please contact BTA, 1190 Saratoga Avenue, #150, San Jose, CA 95129; (408) 244-7852. While these herbs grow only in Nigeria and Ethiopia, numerous others can be found all

over Sub-Saharan Africa—possible sources of drugs to fight the
following:

- ✓ malaria
- ✓ parasitic diseases
- ✓ diarrhea
- ✓ infectious diseases
- ✓ AIDS and related infections
- ✓ cardiovascular diseases
- ✓ respiratory diseases
- ✓ hepatitis
- ✓ mental disorders

Tables 4e and 4f demonstrate that African herbs exhibit superior
healing characteristics.

	Liberia	Ghana	Sierra Leone	Nigeria	Senegal	Togo
Malaria	x	x	x	x	x	x
Parasitic diseases	x	x	x	x	x	x
Diarrhea	x	x	x	x	x	x
Infectious diseases	x	x	x	x	x	x
AIDS	x	x	x	x	x	x
Cardiovascular Diseases	x	x	x	x	x	x
Respiratory Diseases	x	x	x	x	x	x
Hepatitis	x	x	x	x	x	x
Mental disorders	x	x	x	x	x	x

Table 4e. Illnesses Treated with Sub-Saharan Herbs: Part 1.

	Kenya	Uganda	Ethiopia	Cameroon
Malaria	x	x	x	x
Parasitic diseases	x	x	x	x
Diarrhea	x	x	x	x
Infectious diseases	x	x	x	x
AIDS	x	x	x	x
Cardiovascular diseases	x	x	x	x
Respiratory diseases	x	x	x	x
Hepatitis	x	x	x	x
Mental disorders	x	x	x	x

Table 4f. Illnesses Treated with Sub-Saharan Herbs: Part 2.

Herbs as Treatment for Radiation Poisoning

After the Second World War, many Western countries began to test nuclear weapons. The French government, for example, conducted numerous tests in the Sahara. Electrons emitted from radioactive isotopes from the nuclear blast mixed with atmospheric dust and scattered throughout some parts of Nigeria, causing the following conditions in the people living in those areas:

> Stochastic: This is function of dose without threshold, such as neoplastic disease (late effects).

> Nonstochastic: This is when the severity of effects depends on the dose, and for which a threshold may occur, such as early effects (fatigue, nausea, vomiting, etc.).

Data about the use of black soap—or black African soap—to treat radiation sickness is provided in table 4g. Around 1970, the number of deaths due to radiation poisoning dropped significantly as more people became aware of the protective power of black soap around 1970. Black soap is made from African herbs.

Test Year	Roentgens Dispersed	# of Exposed People	# of Deaths
1966	450–500	25,000	1,683
1967	500–600	28,470	1,042
1968	600–650	27,400	642
1969	600–675	20,910	320
1970	675–700	34,547	104

Table 4g. "Black Soap" treatment against radiation poisoning as documented by Nigerian clinical registry

If black soap is effective against beta and gamma radiation, which is more damaging to the body than are cancer or AIDS, then it may also contain the following:

- ✓ thiol radio protector
- ✓ transdermal free radical scavenger
- ✓ surfactants and metal chelating

These unique characteristics of black soap make it an effective treatment against poisoning associated with the following:

UV-B Radiation
The stratospheric ozone layer over the Antarctic has declined sharply over the last decade, and the depletion is expected to continue. This depletion has allowed enhanced penetration of UV-B radiation to the earth's surface where UV-B radiation has been historically low. Even a small increase in ambient UV-B radiation can cause serious skin cancer and other skin problems. Black soap, with its pharmaceutical properties, could be used as a cost-effective treatment for and protection against skin cancer and other skin diseases associated with UV-B.

Radiation in Space

Radiation exposure may not currently pose a significant problem for astronauts taking a short trip in the space shuttle, characterized by a low-earth orbit and traveling about five to ten milliards per day. (A milliard is one thousand million.) This situation is likely to change as use of the space station increases.

Comprehensive radiobiological review of the physical interactions and transport of space radiation (protons, electrons, and galactic heavy ions) show that high-energy ions (HZE particles) may be highly carcinogenic during a prolonged space mission. This is of particular concern, as it means an increasing number of astronauts will be exposed to the radiation field that exists when they are in an orbit of about 450–500 kilometers high and an inclination of about 28.5 degrees for extended period of time. The radiation-shielding or radiation-absorbing elements in black soap has been used in a variety of applications. Based upon its extraordinary protective measures against radiation poisoning, it would be advantageous to evaluate black soap as a cost-effective alternative medicine.

Bone Demineralization

The biological implications of bone demineralization—which results from aging, prolonged weightlessness, and radiation—have not been well investigated. As a result, no effective countermeasures have been developed. For many centuries, physicians used prolonged bed rest and immersion in water as treatment for various diseases, especially in Sub-Saharan Africa, where access to medical technology was lacking. These treatments had positive effects, that is, until patients returned to their daily activities. Studies on these changes and their effects indicate that:

During bed rest, abrupt changes in position cause acute changes in the body's fluid compartments, which affect

- ✓ renal function,
- ✓ calcium and phosphorus metabolism, and
- ✓ orthostatic tolerance and bone demineralization.

During water immersion, abrupt changes in position cause acute changes in the body's fluid compartments, which affect

- ✓ cardiovascular-respiratory responses,
- ✓ natriuretic and diuretic factors,
- ✓ renal function, and
- ✓ bone demineralization.

A significant percentage of Africans used butter derived from African herbs as treatment against fatigue and muscle weakness. Using radiographic and clinical evaluations, physicians determined that Africans using the herb-based butter before submitting to bed rest and water immersion did not experience bone demineralization or any associated symptoms. That was in marked contrast to those who did not use that butter. Another African bone demineralization-related experience during the French nuclear testing in the Sahara, which emitted radioactive particles across West Africa, including to Nigeria and Ghana. The medical community accepts that no topical treatment can reduce the effect of gamma radiation on the bones, However, the chemical characteristics of herb-based butter may prove otherwise.

Chapter 5

The Fall of Black Civilization

All modern scientific, technological, and medical advancements arose from early research and inventions. For example, aviation technology is based on the work done by the Wright brothers and automobile technology is based on efforts by Henry Ford. In the same way, modern advancements in medical technology are based on the work of early researchers, who neither surveyed nor examined members of the black race. Given this situation, it is safe to conclude that early medical research efforts had a negative impact on the treatment of black people.

All chronic conditions, and their associated serious illnesses, have been attributed to the black race. How accurate are these assessments? To perform a convincing analysis, we will compare the natural resources of Sub-Saharan nations to those of the industrialized nations. The location of Sub-Saharan Africa is a big advantage, given the favorable climate with sufficient rainfall all the year round. It is therefore safe to say that Sub-Saharan nations can grow and produce healthier crops than the industrialized world can.

The consumption of food in the industrialized world, including the United States, hit a peak due to a rapid population increase. But it is now on the way down, which has created a glut in the global food market. The anticipated food shortage associated with this phenomenon encouraged farmers to grow genetically engineered crops to meet the growing demand. This led to chronic conditions and various other serious illnesses that sent a high percentage of people to the hospital; many died from their illnesses. The treatment of those who were hospitalized costs several hundred million dollars a year, compromising the health care budget.

There is therefore an urgent need to produce and supply healthier food products, which means those that have not been genetically engineered and lack artificial ingredients. Meeting this demand, especially in the United States, is expected to pose a serious financial burden on low-income working families. It could further deplete the food supply in the industrialized world. Given this situation, one can now factor the agricultural resources of Sub-Saharan nations into the food supply equation to determine the pivotal role they will play in creating sustainable and dependable food products with healthy and natural ingredients.

Without adequate investment in agricultural tools and machinery, it will be very difficult for African farmers to capitalize on this specific golden opportunity, which did not exist several decades ago. At this time, Sub-Saharan Africa is at both social and economic crossroad. Its crops could be responsible for a variety of health advantages. Black Africans enjoy more healthy advantages than other ethnicities do. Because of the quality of their food, they enjoy the following advantages:

- ✓ look younger than other groups
- ✓ few or no hospital visits in a lifetime
- ✓ ability to age gracefully
- ✓ longer life spans (ninety to one hundred years old)

My grandmother never visited any hospital during her lifetime, yet she passed away at the age of ninety. Most black Africans, especially those in the rural areas, enjoy life spans of more than a hundred years. This superior health advantage can be attributed to their superior diet, which gives them plenty of energy and the ability to think on their feet. Yet, many black Africans still experience the following problems:

- ✓ starvation and malnourishment
- ✓ poverty
- ✓ underemployment
- ✓ poor access to the health care system
- ✓ a weak economy

Some of these problems can be attributed to limited skills and the lack of tools required for mechanized farming. Only through mechanized farming will Sub-Saharan Africans achieve mass production of their agricultural products. Without mechanized farming, production will be maintained at a local level, which could compromise production and affect economic output.

Can Africans enjoy quality health care in the twenty-first century, after more than one hundred years of being denied access to it? Before colonization, black people were physically fit, due to the health advantages discussed above. The colonization of Sub-Saharan Africa marked a miserable turning point for black people in terms of their overall and economic conditions. Given that Sub-Saharan Africans used a bow-and-arrow defense against their colonizers, they were defeated. As a result, they were forced to abandon their traditional remedies and embrace the medicine introduced by the colonizers. Colonization killed Sub-Saharan civilization by excluding black people from every decision-making process, including those related to medical research.

Key Sub-Saharan Weapons
These assessments make it very difficult for any physician, regardless of qualifications or experience, to give a satisfactory diagnosis and prescribe effective medication or treatment to a black person without trial and error. I have often wondered why no black person has come forward to challenge most of the baseless and unverifiable medical findings about the black community. After all, there are qualified black doctors.

After a careful examination of the facts and some logical analysis, I realized that, regardless of the education and skills they acquire, black scientists and doctors cannot challenge any of these deficient reports regarding the black race. This is due to the fact that their education is still based on early research that excluded the black population. As a result, black people, regardless of their economic status, will continue to accept whatever their doctors tell them.

For example, the claim that black people, particularly black men, have high blood pressure, should be subject to scientific investigation. I make this argument based on the fact that the research on which such information was based did not include data from the black population. Without that, no medical professional can document with any certainty any of the disorders attributed to black people all over the world.

Are the disorders associated with black people based on a scientific findings or are they part of a strategic plot to intimidate and humiliate the black race? Either way, there are no scientific data to justify such claims.

I once asked a highly respected medical professional for her thoughts on black people and high blood pressure, as it is currently documented in the medical literature. She told me in very simple terms that to her best knowledge, high blood pressure is related to an unknown mechanism for conservation of water in hot climate. Because large part of Sub-Saharan Africa is located along the equator, she continued, it was believed that black people conserve high volumes of water in hot climate; therefore, they must exhibit symptoms of high blood pressure. She concluded that, based on these facts, high blood pressure was attributed to skin color. She said that is probably the reason why the medical community found that black people, particularly black men, have high blood pressure.

Is that proof? You can answer the question better than I can. If you go through the key medical findings and see how such findings were made, you probably will be shocked. The fact is, no accurate medical diagnoses currently exist to justify the finding that black people, particularly black men, have high blood pressure and are more likely to suffer heart attacks.

By the way, is high blood pressure genetic or acquired via the environment? If it is not inherited, then African slaves did not exhibit any symptoms of high blood pressure when they were brought to this country. Were African slaves diagnosed with high-blood-pressure when they arrived in the United States? I think not. Were the people living in Africa diagnosed with high blood pressure at the time of the slave trade? Again, I think not.

As discussed in chapter 4, Sub-Saharan Africa has a very favorable climate all year round, which gives it the enormous advantage of being able to grow healthier crops compared to other parts of the world. As a result, Africans eat healthy, unlike the United States and other industrialized countries.

Could artificial ingredients create or cause high blood pressure? Even if that is true, the claim that black people are mostly associated with high blood pressure is still questionable. The primary problem with the medical treatment of black people is that it is questionable, because the research on which it is based was conducted without any statistical data from the black population. The blood pressure reading system is not an expectation. How can such instrument be used to accurately read the blood pressure of black people? One could argue if the system works for other ethnic groups, why not for black people. The answer is simple: because their biological composition differs considerably; otherwise we all would be just one color.

Can misdiagnoses create serious medical problems? You bet, they can. Once a doctor tells you that you are sick, you start feel sick immediately, whether or not you are. That is psychology 101, and such an experience certainly be intimidating.

Chapter 6

Opposing Motion against the Black Race

This chapter examines the level of knowledge, skills, expertise, and apparatus available to black people seeking to successfully develop profitable technologies. The results of the examination will determine if an educational program is an appropriate way to enhance critical thinking, problem-solving, and decision-making skills.

Mineral Resources
The major challenge facing the African mineral industry is the ability to respond to a highly volatile and fragmented market demand by rapidly launching new products that will be profitable and offer advantages in science and technology. The expertise and knowledge needed for this complex undertaking include the following types of engineering:

- ✓ metallurgical
- ✓ mining
- ✓ petroleum
- ✓ chemical
- ✓ geological

Table 6a was compiled using data from the US Department of Commerce's Housing and Household Economic Statistics Division. It compares the qualifications of black people to the scientific knowhow required to launch new technologies from these resources.

	General	White	Black	White %	Black %
Population	267,000,000	219,600,000	33,600,000	82%	13%
Metallurgical	19,000	17,000	665	90%	3%
Mining	6,500	6,000	68	94%	1%
Petroleum	24,000	23,000	539	93%	2%

Chemical	64,300	57,000	2,200	89%	4%
Geological	53,000	51,000	604	96%	1%

Table 6a. The scientific and technological capabilities of white people and black people in the United States to develop technologies from the African mineral resources.

The figures in table 6a show that of nineteen thousand metallurgical engineers in the United States, only 665 (3 percent) are black, and 17,000 (90 percent) are white. Of 6,500 mining engineers, only 68 (1 percent) are black, and 6,000 (94 percent) are white. Of 24,000 petroleum engineers, only 539 (2 percent) are black, and 23,000 (93 percent) are white. Of 64,000 chemical engineers, only 2,200 (4 percent) are black, and 57,000 (89 percent) are white. Of 53,000 geological engineers, only 604 (1 percent) are black, and 51,000 (96 percent) are white.

Agricultural Resources
The ability of Sub-Saharan Africa to respond to the highly volatile and fragmented market will require improved knowledge in science and technology. This may not be that challenging because Africans have been involved in agriculture since the beginning of time. However, in Africa, cultivation has been on a comparatively smaller scale. Expanding agricultural production will require additional expertise and knowhow, including the following:

✓ agricultural and food scientists
✓ biological and life scientists
✓ forestry and conservation scientists
✓ agricultural engineers

Table 6b was compiled using data from the US Department of Commerce's Housing and Household Economic Statistics Division. It compares the qualifications of black people against the scientific knowhow required to successfully export African agricultural products on a large scale.

	General	White	Black	White %	Black %
Population	267,000,000	219,600,000	33,600,000	82%	13%
Agriculture & food scientists	35,000	32,000	1,500	91%	4%
Biological & life scientists	62,000	54,400	2,4003	88%	4%
Forestry & conservation scientists	34,800	32,500	1,100	93%	3%
Agricultural engineers	2,400	2,000	45	93%	2%

Table 6b. The scientific and technological capabilities of white and black people in the United States to developing African agricultural products into a large export market.

Plant-Based Medicinal Products

The major challenge facing the Sub-Saharan pharmaceutical and biotechnology industry is convincing the world health care industry that African herbs have remarkable healing properties and should be used to produce medicines for global consumption. Certainly, it will be difficult for black people to carry this burden, considering their limited expertise in this area. Does this mean that black people should abandon their desire to gain superior economic status in the twenty-first century? Definitely not! It simply means that they will face challenging and complex problems on the path to economic revolution.

How will black people tackle these problems? There are two answers to this question. One answer, which is not in the best business interests of black people, is to invite international funders to invest heavily in research and development. However, this means that black people still will be dependent on foreign investors and competitors, who may take more than 50 percent of the profits. The second answer is to establish comprehensive educational programs. Only through education will black people be able to acquire the skills and expertise they need. The development of educational programs to train people in science and technology adds additional complications. Black Technologies Advancement has developed strategies to help black people meet the challenges they face in this area.

Today, African minerals are controlled by a fragmented system. Each country has unique methods of research and documentation. The lack of an adequate infrastructure is a costly obstacle. There is also a need to maintain high-quality systems engineering to ensure reliability, availability, maintainability, and data integrity as well as a high level of confidence needed to produce products in the most cost-effective manner. Black Technologies Advancement's program is incorporates recent advances in information technology as they apply to Sub-Sahara natural resources to improve the economic status of black people.

Chapter 7

Serious Diseases in the Black Community

White people have fewer diseases than other groups. This is because early medical research was based on studies of the white race.

Any serious or life-threatening illness or diseases of major concern to society usually are associated with black people. "African American Health Facts," a 1997 report issued by the Office of Minority Health Resource Center in Washington, DC, cites the *Monthly Vital Statistics Report* 45, no. 3 (National Center for Health Statistics, Advance Report of Final Mortality Statistics, September 30, 1996) to state the top ten leading causes of death among African Americans in 1994 were the following:

1. Heart disease (27.2 percent)
2. Cancer (21.2 percent)
3. Stroke (6.4 percent)
4. HIV infection (5.7 percent)
5. Unintentional injuries (4.5 percent)
6. Homicide 4.3%
7. Diabetes (3.5 percent)
8. Pneumonia/influenza (2.6 percent)
9. Chronic obstructive pulmonary disease (2.3 percent)
10. Perinatal conditions (2 percent)

These particular facts were further well documented by "The Empowerment Initiative" (TEI), a bimonthly newsletter geared toward empowering African Americans.

In addition to the ten diseases listed, black women are now associated with breast cancer. According to recent medical literature, black women are more likely to suffer from breast cancer than all other ethnic groups put together. Furthermore, cancer is documented as the second-leading cause of death for black people, who have a higher age-adjusted death rate than any other racial group. The statistical breakdown reads as follows: between 1973 and 1991, cancer mortality for white males increased by only 5.6 percent, but it increased by 24 percent for black males. The rate increased by 13.3 percent for black women and only 8.1 percent for white women. How were these statistical data compiled?

It is undocumented medical fact that black people usually do not suffer from melanoma. Otherwise, black Africans would be dying every second of the day from melanoma caused by the intense high temperature from the sun. Is there any scientific or medical proof to justify this idea that blacks are more likely to suffer from cancer than other races? If so, on what medical logic was the study based? Was testing involved? What equipment was used for the study? How was this testing equipment developed? Did any black people participate in the studies? These are the questions black people should ask themselves whenever they are diagnosed with any of the above-mentioned illnesses. It is very disappointing when people accept medical findings without challenging the data.

Studies indicate that many African Americans are at high risk for HIV infection—not because of their race or ethnicity but because of the risky behaviors in which they may engage. We all know that the children of poor parents are subject to serious economic problems that may force them to use drugs and alcohol, which encourages unsafe sex behavior. A shortage of employment opportunities means there is nothing to occupy their time except drinking and drug use. Drugs and alcohol are triggers for unsafe sex behaviors, which create the prime conditions for the AIDS/HIV virus.

No matter what ethnic group you belong to, it is not who you are but what you do that puts you at risk for AIDS and HIV. It has been documented that African Americans are disproportionately affected by AIDS, compared to other races, because African Americans account for 33 percent of all the cases in the United States, although black people comprise only 13 percent of the US population. In 1994, 57 percent of women with AIDS were African American. Similarly, African Americans accounted for more than half of all AIDS cases among injecting drug users (IDUs). In 1994, 62 percent of all children with AIDS were African American. What the study did not say is that a variety of groups were included under the "African American" heading—lower class, Christian, Muslim, inner-city, suburban, descendants of slaves, and recent Caribbean immigrants. Why did it fail to record these social, cultural, economic, geographic, religious, and political differences, and thus document accurate statistics regarding the black population? It is an established fact that high numbers of black people are affected by AIDS/HIV, but it is unfair to put them with other groups to make them think otherwise. Scientists in Sub-Saharan Africa have made impressive headways in developing effective countermeasures against AIDS/HIV. However, they experience major difficulties due to lack of funding.

In 2000, former US vice president Al Gore was challenged by AIDS/HIV advocates during his presidential campaign kickoff in his hometown, because he had failed to support efforts to fund to research black Africans with AIDS/HIV. In 1993, local, state, and territory health departments reported to the Centers for Disease Control that there were 58,538 cases of AIDS among racial/ethnic minorities. A total of 38,544 (66 percent) cases were reported among black people, 18,888 (32 percent) among Latinos, 767 (1 percent) among people of Asian / Pacific Islander descent, and 339 (1 percent) among America Indians / Alaskan natives. Data about white population were not included.

We can employ this specific analogy to reevaluate the funding for high blood pressure, cancer, and other serious illnesses attributed to black people.

Chapter 8

Black Patients and Doctors

The isolation of the black population from early medical research continues to isolate them from satisfactory medical treatments or cures. Doctors, particularly white doctors, still have difficulties providing quality or comprehensive health care services to black people.

The patient-doctor relationship, especially the interaction between black patients and their doctors, should be of concern to the medical community. Chapter 7 stated that serious and life-threatening illnesses are always attributed to black people. Yet no attempt has been made to improve the black patient–doctor relationship. We all know that quality health care is the prerequisite for good health, because when you are in good health, you have peace of mind. Good health and peace of mind are the most important facts of life.

Before we proceed further with this chapter, we need to define *patient*, as used in this book. A patient is someone who

- ✓ is admitted into a hospital for an overnight or extended stay,
- ✓ visits a doctor for a one-time exam, or
- ✓ visits the doctor for regular medical checkup.

Now, we can examine the relationship between a black patient and his doctor and a white patient and his doctor. This will allow us to determine which is the most unfavorable relationship.

In most cases, the black patient–doctor relationship has been very unfavorable to patients and needs to improve if black people can ever enjoy any improved health care benefits. The relationship might be negatively affected because of the doctor's views about black people. Regardless of how wealthy and successful a black person is, he or she is still black. No one can change that simple fact. The relationship may be compromised because black people do not command any influence in the medical profession. The doctor may not have the necessary data regarding the health of black people. Such information is needed to accurately assess and treat a patient, particularly when the illness is unique and life threatening.

When, a black person suffers from a unique type of illnesses, there is a greater likelihood that doctors will employ trial-and-error techniques to determine an effective treatment. In such situations, the patient may experience additional illnesses due to side effects. In other words, while the doctor is trying to achieve a cure, he or she might be making the black patient sicker.

Let us now examine the white patient–doctor relationship, which is the most favorable relationship, in part because in most cases the doctor—who is usually white—understands the biological makeup of other white people. The doctor knows exactly how to perform an accurate assessment of white patients. If the doctor is from another ethnic group, the white patient will still enjoy a favorable patient-doctor relationship. This is because the doctor's training was based on data about the white population. One can say, therefore, that white people enjoy every medical advantage not only in the United States but in other parts of the world.

Chapter 9

Black People and the News Media

Why don't black people help each other? That is a good question. Here is another: why aren't black people united? And a third: why are black people afraid to trust one another? Finally, why is there so little teamwork and unity among black people today? The correct answers to these questions can be found in the news media, which confuses black people to such an extent that they do not trust one another.

While studies have shown otherwise, in my opinion the news media has convinced black people that they are inferior to other races. This inferiority complex has existed since the news media first launched its negative publicity against the black race. Why the news media is against black people is not known. However, slavery and colonization might have been the influencing factor.

It is said that birds of a feather flock together. If this saying can be applied to any race, it definitely is appropriate for the black race. This is because of problems created by the news media. The image of black people as created by the news media is very discouraging, especially to the black youth. As a result, too many black children want to be athletes or entertainers, because that is all they see when they watch the television.

Frankly speaking, black entertainers and athletes—who are not knowledgeable in science, technology, or medicine—do not do anything to address this particular problem among Blacks. Many of them refuse to support the few black people involved in science, technology, and medicine.

Let us now revisit one of the questions posed at the beginning of this chapter: why are black people afraid to trust one another? It could be due to black entertainers and athletes' limited knowledge about science, technology, or medicine. This might be compounded by the negative image of black people created by the news media.

Consequently, black people with the potential to create a better economic environment for others have refused to do so, because they believe that few black scientists will take advantage of their investment. Entertainers and athletes believe that the black scientists will use any money they receive dishonestly. This belief is based upon the limited engineering or scientific knowledge of the entertainers and the athletes. Subsequently, well-qualified black scientists, especially those who own hi-tech small businesses, find it very difficult to generate any money from black entertainers or athletes.

As a result, black-owned hi-tech companies with demonstrated track records struggle to generate the capital to expand their businesses and create more employment opportunities. One of the ways black people can be identified with science, technology, or medicine in the twenty-first century will be through the ownership of profitable and successful hi-tech businesses that rely on African natural resources; collaborations between black Africans and African Americans; and support from black entertainers and athletes. This is frustrating scenario because black people with innovative ideas often are unable to act on those ideas and take them to the market place. This is due, in part, to their inability to generate the funds they need.

The challenge lies in our ability to encourage black children to become scientists, engineers, and doctors rather than entertainers or athletes. Creating financial opportunities for black scientists will enable them to demonstrate their ideas and create successful commercial products. Creating such opportunities will be very difficult due, as stated already, to the problems in generating the necessary funding.

The negative publicity that arises from the news media complicates the problem further. A well-designed, mapped-out strategy can help black scientists launched their careers in the twenty-first century. Any effective plan will involve grass-roots education and a well-organized network. Without such a strategy, there will be complications.

Chapter 10

Is Prayer the Answer to the Problem?

As I stated in my poem about the struggling boy, if any race should be commended for worship or prayer, it is the black race. Even so, black people in the world today still face serious economic problems. Has anyone in the black community—or anyone from any other race, for that matter—ever wondered why this is the case? If black people are still facing terrible financial problems, then they must not be worshiping according to the rules set forth by God.

Several decades ago, African Americans experienced terrible social and civil rights violations, and black Africans were oppressed by the white governments that colonized them. Black people were concerned about these sad situations and wanted to end the oppression. They prayed for an immediate end to this sad experience. God answered their prayers by giving them prominent leaders who worked to end these tragedies. The leader for African Americans in this crusade was Martin Luther King Jr. God blessed King with the wisdom he needed to lead this crusade. Although he lost his life, his mission was accomplished. He gave black people the social equality they deserved.

Africa's leader in this crusade was Dr. Nnamdi Azikiwe. His experience with the social injustice in the United States influenced his assumption of a leadership role in Africa. When he returned to Nigeria in 1958/59 after completing his education in the United States, Azikiwe decided to expel all the white people from his country. His mission was successful, because in 1960 he secured independence for Nigeria from the British, and Azikiwe became the first Nigerian president. In the subsequent years, other African countries became independent as well. I offer this narrative with great confidence, because during my stay in Dakar, Senegal, I was cared for by Azikiwe's houseboy who devoted much time to me. While Azikiwe motivated King to lead the crusade in the United States, King's name has become world famous, while that of Dr.

Azikiwe remained in obscurity, due to information distributed by the news media.

However, this chapter will investigate why the black race faces the worst economic problems in the world despite their vigorous worshiping activities and praying power. Black people's prayers to end the social injustice were answered, but their prayers to end their economic struggle have not been. They succeeded as a team that one time for the following reasons:

- ✓ They specifically identified the problem.
- ✓ They formed specific plans for solving the problem.
- ✓ They were united in a common cause
- ✓ They had a burning desire to achieve a specific goal
- ✓ They had designated leaders and united behind them in a common purpose.
- ✓ They prayed that they would achieve that goal.

Black people ended the oppression with astonishing results in the quickest possible time. If the same techniques and methodologies can be applied to the economy, the financial problems of black people soon would come to an end as well. Unfortunately, there are no plans in place to solve the problem of poverty in the black community. The approach at the moment is to complain and complain. Realistically, no amount of complaints can resolve this problem. Rather, they will make the problem worse.

First, we must correctly identify the cause of the problem. If black people will ever be identified with science, medicine, or technology, they first must be convinced that their financial problems originate from their inability to be identified with such endeavors. Since this is the first time such an argument is being made, it will be difficult to win a majority of supporters, unless the effort is directed by a knowledgeable leader. This leader not only will be knowledgeable about what science, medical, or technology careers will best suit black people, he also will be dedicated with a burning desire and unshakeable commitment to resolve their financial problems.

This unshakeable commitment will be measured by the extent this leader is willing to go in order to succeed. He will undertake a major grassroots crusade to educate Black communities regarding the specific causes of action to resolve this devastating problem. This crusade will unite the black race as a team with a common cause. This team effort likely will convince and motivate wealthy black individuals to provide the necessary financial support necessary to successfully launch the crusade. Otherwise, it will be very difficult to succeed in this effort; black people's economic security will remain in jeopardy; and they will continue to feel inferior for an extended period of time.

Given these facts, the black race now can pray or worship with a defined purpose: solving their financial problems. Prayers without a specified purpose usually go unanswered, but prayers with defined purpose are always answered. You must know what you want before you ask for it. If you do not say precisely what you want, people do not know what to give you.

One reason why people's prayers have not been answered is that no one in the black community has tried to find out why black people face the worst economic problems in the world today. The reason is that they are not identified with science, technology, or medicine, which equal economic security. This methodology of hope is the prerequisite for economic security.

Therefore, identifying black people with science, technology, and medicine is the prerequisite for economic prosperity. Several arenas are appropriate for black involvement, but specific activities will give black people a head start on achieving the following:

- ✓ superior economic power
- ✓ domestic and international prestige
- ✓ improved academic status in science, technology, and medicine

Appropriate science, technology, and medical products must come from Africa. The resources discussed in chapter 2 have everything that will give the black race what it needs.

Chapter 11

Bridging the Agricultural Gap

This chapter discusses solutions for the challenges that threaten Sub-Saharan agriculture. Recent events have raised questions about why, despite decades of effort, Sub-Saharan Africa remains impoverished. Africa is poorer today than it was in 1960, in some places by a wide margin. As a result, Sub-Saharan nations have been subject to large-scale experiments to reform their economies. However ambitious, these projects have failed to generate sustained economic growth. Sub-Saharan Africa—with its abundant natural resources, including crude oil, and a highly skilled labor force—is the most prosperous region on the continent, yet its citizens are starved and malnourished. Performing molecular manipulations by manipulating electrical, magnetic, optical, mechanical, and other physical properties of African minerals provide opportunities to develop food and water safety with a significant impact on rural populations using advanced renewable energy technologies, namely wind energy. Through the integration of these molecular properties, we will address key technological limitations that prevent the deployment of wind turbine blades with coded expert knowledge to meet the food security demand for this region.

Designing highly efficient nanocomposites—that is, pure carbon fibers with nanotubes exhibiting mechanical, electrical, thermal, and barrier properties suitable for wind-turbine blades with large rotary radii with integrated chips in the form of coded expert knowledge with 3-D nanostructuring and coding—can provide the required intelligence to the blade systems to set and adjust the blade aerodynamic behavior to perform the required tasks.

Integrating Sub-Saharan African resources with nanotechnology offers a significant opportunity to develop agriculture in this region. The greatest challenge facing the agricultural sector is the delivery of useful information to rural communities. Training programs for farmers and recycling establishments are entirely possible, given the advances in computer technology, which can be used to support agricultural activities. With the unlimited growth of the Internet, we can create a learning infrastructure that will equip rural farmers with valuable information about how to maximize production. The training program should incorporate key players in the agricultural sector by addressing their information requirements, as shown in table 11b. Using the extensive contributions to the field by agricultural scientists, we can identify farmers' specific information needs as shown in table 11c.

This program will focus mainly on rural farmers, as shown in table 11d. This is because they need to learn about the techniques and methods that enhance crop production, streamline the harvest, and help them market their products successfully. Traditional approaches encouraged farmers to obtain information from colleagues, community leaders, the press, demonstrations, and exhibitions. To a great extent, these approaches have been unsuccessful. My program changes the dynamics and equips farmers with the skills and expertise to maximize their productivity. (See the six modules presented in table 11d and the work plan.)

Program Description

The program will address the comprehensive benefits of the program to rural farmers, including the production of solid-waste recyclables and compost, as shown in table 11a.

Program	*Program Objectives*
Business and financial advice	Evaluation of the viability of customer enterprises assets and operations through experienced financial analysis, including cost of services and insurances rates.
Facility planning, permits, and design	Development of solid-waste facilities requires an interdisciplinary process and engineering expertise. We will offer customers project teams that have experience composting all types of solid waste to improve crop cultivation

Hazardous materials management	Industrial and solid-waste streams contain hazardous materials that may threaten human health and the environment. We will show customers how to dispose of hazardous materials, respond to regulatory requirements, and safeguard their communities.
Operations and performance enhancement	Competitive pressures and demands for higher efficiency at lower costs pose challenges to organizations dealing in solid waste. Our operations and performance-enhancement services will help companies thrive in the solid-waste marketplace
Recycling program design and promotion	We will design recycling programs and help clients market their recyclable materials. This includes managing waste as a resource and preserving resources for future generations through materials recovery.
Services procurement	Identifying a solid-waste service provider can be complicated and challenging. This project offers strategies and solutions for hiring a company to provide a comprehensive set of services, such as collection, processing, long-haul transport, and disposal.
Waste-management and sustainability planning	Strategies targeting sustainable composting derived from solid waste integrate community needs with technical, financial, regulatory, social, and environmental requirements. We will deliver innovative solutions based on effective, integrated planning.

Table 11a. Training Program.

The program will highlight agricultural opportunities, practices, innovations, limitations, successes, and trends. It will address the growing consensus within the farming industry that farmers have not used natural composting to benefit their communities in the following ways:

- ✓ reduce or eliminate the need for chemical fertilizers
- ✓ promote higher yields of agricultural crops
- ✓ facilitate reforestation, wetlands restoration, and habitat revitalization efforts by amending contaminated, compacted, and marginal soils
- ✓ use cost-effective remediate soils contaminated by hazardous waste
- ✓ avoid methane and leachate formulation in landfills
- ✓ save at least 50 percent more than conventional soil, water, and air pollution remediation techniques, where applicable
- ✓ reduce the need for water, fertilizer, and pesticides
- ✓ serves as a marketable community and as a low-cost alternative to standard landfill cover and artificial soil amendments

Program Objectives

This program trains rural farmers to produce, process, and distribute food, using applicable scientific and technical data. It helps farmers to improve the quantity and quality of their crops, which are indispensable to human life. It is offered at different levels—from children's classes in village schools to graduate-level study in universities. Education and training are widely acknowledged as important contributors to national economic development and social well-being. Agricultural training programs usually focus on more diverse objectives. This program helps farmers acquire skills in crop production, animal husbandry, water management, soil cultivation, pesticide/herbicide application, nitrogen-based nutrition. The training program modules proposed will be applicable to agricultural support subsystem.

Participant Objectives

The program will address the information needs of key players, including agricultural scientists, as shown in tables 11b and 11c. However, this program focuses mainly on rural farmers, because of their desperate need for information about how to improve their productivity; see table 11d.

User Population	Information Needs
Policy makers	Production levels, resource use, market outlook, state and national outlook
Research and industrial scientists	Immediate access to the latest research, standards, techniques, procedures, patent and product details, trade information, market outlook
Special advisors, extension personnel	Immediate access to the latest research, standards, techniques, procedures, patent and product details, trade information, market outlook
Educators	Current practices and issues, computer literacy
Agricultural service industry	Market trends, production estimates, prospects for the industry, research results, new practices, government policy, rapid access to new information
Consumers (farmers, ranchers, and rural residents)	Production, marketing, and consumer data, information to help people manage their lives and cope with everyday problems

Table 11b. Information Needs of the Agricultural Sector.

User Population	Information Needs
Agricultural scientists	Production techniques and levels, resource use, market outlook, rapid access to latest research and researchers, current practices
Remarks	Although these are not necessarily the needs of farmers, they do reflect the common interests of the agricultural sector. Farmers throughout the world are constantly searching for ways to maximize their returns. Our proposed web-based system will provide the technology farmers need to maximize the economic and environmental benefits of farming. Unfortunately, most farmers do not have the access to the information they need. Through this process, information will be shared by scientists and large and small farmers.

Table 11c. Information Needs of Agricultural Scientists.

Program Modules	Program Objectives
Module 1: Correct farming techniques	Farmers learn the techniques that will maximize productivity.
Module 2: Techniques for planting correct crops	Farmers are given an environmental analysis that will aid the planting of correct crops
Module 3: Harvesting methods to maximize productivity	Farmers receive information on developing harvesting techniques to maximize productivity
Module 4: Marketing and entrepreneurial skills	Farmers learn how to identify the techniques and strategies that will help them sustain the viability of customer enterprises assets, and operations through experienced financial analysis.
Modules 5: Computer skills	Computers are useful tools for agricultural support because they give farmers better access to farming technology, which makes their farming more efficient. In addition, farmers can use computers to access marketing information from online databases focused on agricultural commodities. In the short term, this will help them to decide where and when to market their produce. In the long term, it will help them to decide what crops to plant.
Modules 6: Appropriate soft skills	Farmers are given information on developing soft skills.

Table 11d. Information Needs of Rural Farmers.

Program Goals

Rural farmers need information about techniques that can improve crop production and how to harvest and market those crops successfully. Various initiatives have been undertaken to address these needs, often with the goal of enhancing local and national economies.

In 1986, the US Department of Agriculture identified the agricultural sector as the country's biggest industry and the largest employer. Information available in the literature tends to support the view that most of the above-mentioned initiatives were traditional approaches. They encouraged farmers to rely on colleagues, community leaders, the popular press, demonstrations, and exhibitions to provide information. To a great extent, these approaches have not been successful. As a result, other approaches are emerging—mainly based on the use of technology. Proponents of this approach explain that information technology is relevant in rural areas since it reduces the cost of acquiring information, is relatively easy to use, and can provide faster access.

State-of-the-Art
The greatest challenge facing the agricultural sector is the delivery of useful information to rural communities. Rural communities in California, for example, have a growing population, sparsely distributed families, minority groups, deprived households, a short supply of information sources, long distances to travel, remote commercial facilities, lack of proper life-support systems, high education–related expenditures, low educational achievements, and low family incomes. One way to improve crop production is to reduce the gap between theory and practice; that can happen only if correct methods of communication are implemented. Such methods should support both direct and indirect communication. Before the emergence of the Internet, no medium offered an opportunity to utilize both ways of communication.

In the last few years, the World Wide Web has created positive possibilities in communication, particularly in rural communities, which are plagued by a lack of access to information. Because of its ability to allow both methods of communication at a relatively cheap cost, the web is seen crucial for bridging the information gap. To provide a basis for the actual design of a web-based information center, it first is necessary to understand the characteristics of rural communities. Otherwise, it will not be possible to provide appropriate solutions. As noted above, rural farmers seek information about the techniques that can assist their work. They are looking for more than traditional approaches, which have been largely unsuccessful. Instead, they are turning to technology in their search for information. The black community lacks qualified workers with the technical and soft skills to adapt to technological and scientific change. Yet, companies are experiencing a lack of qualified workers in the areas of Windows and Java programming and systems and database administration.

Many of the world's emerging industries, particularly those in the United States, seek employees with technical skills that were not needed only a few years ago. In addition, many corporations have come to value the "soft skills"—that is, independent, creative problem-solving skills, interpersonal and communication skills, critical thinking skills, the ability to adapt to rapid change in technology and science. Many corporations seek to hire black professionals to help them bridge the digital gap, as businesses and nonprofit organizations move from host-centric computer environments to client-server computing architectures and applications. In a recently published white paper, Oracle Corporation stated that among black people around the nation and the world, information technology talent continues to fall short of demand. Black engineers and scientists identified the lack of skills as the most serious constraint on identifying black people with any science- or technology-related products.

A Solution
Bridging the digital gap among blacks will have a regional and a global impact, based on the number of black people who will take advantage of this effort. A curriculum that gives direct access to those interested in bridging the gap in information technology is required for this effort. Such curriculum could serve as a school-to-work program, which will provide the requisite skills that enable black people to design, develop, and market science- and technology-related products. Our goals in this effort are to

- ✓ develop and deliver a rigorous curriculum in information technology;
- ✓ meet the needs of black technology professionals seeking to advance their skills;

✓ train faculty in new education strategies and electronic delivery systems, using industry standards to accommodate a large percentage of the population; and

✓ reach diverse groups of nontraditional students, including those from the black community.

A long-term goal is to provide the complete curriculum on demand—any time, any place, and at any pace—to program participants.

Systemic Reform

In response to industry needs, this effort will develop and implement the following systemic reforms:

✓ Provide a forum in which the industry will work with faculty at academic institutions to develop skills-oriented curricula, including soft skills, that match what black people need to achieve this mission.

✓ Equip program participants with technical skills to perform competitively in the workplace.

✓ Intertwine math, science, and information-technology curricula to allow participants to compete successfully.

✓ Develop internship programs so participants can learn on the job.

✓ Create the information technology skills required by the business sector.

✓ Train faculty how to teach high-performance outcomes at work sites.

✓ Test new teaching techniques and learning outcomes in a computer laboratory.

✓ Increase diversity within the target workforce.

✓ Maintain a clearing house to disseminate research-driven forecasts, education-reform strategies, needs assessments, skill standards, and academic curricula.

Plan of Action

Black Technologies Advancement (BTA) will bring together key partners from education, industry and government to accomplish three goals:

- ✓ Develop the curriculum.
- ✓ Disseminate the curriculum.
- ✓ Provide professional support to develop, revise, and disseminate curriculum.

The initial focus will be to create a comprehensive curriculum in computer science, mathematics, engineering, and information technology. Once the curriculum has been successfully tested, it will serve as a worldwide model not only for instruction over the Internet.

Strategies for Achieving Project Goals

- ✓ Establish job skill sets with input from industry partners.
- ✓ Incorporate soft skills within the curriculum, offer internship experiences for program participants; and certify skill acquisition based upon industry standards
- ✓ Test new teaching techniques and learning outcomes in a computer laboratory.
- ✓ Give the previously underserved black community access to nontraditional teaching and learning environments, such as the Internet.
- ✓ Train faculty how to teach high-performance outcomes at worksites.

We will assemble an advisory board, which will include representatives from corporations, universities, and industries worldwide. With their input, we will outline a curriculum to train high-performing black workers. The advisory board will meet quarterly. BTA will mobilize industry, education, labor, and community leaders to develop

- ✓ educational programs that encourage lifelong learning;
- ✓ a rigorous academic, relevant, career-related curriculum;
- ✓ a comprehensive introduction to the characteristics of a high-performing workplace and how to expand work-based learning opportunities in the black community; and
- ✓ industry-validated standards, a reliable assessment of learning outcomes, and certificates of achievement that indicate what program participants know and can do.

Summary

This project will develop a computer-based, instructional-design tool built on a set of heuristics and guidance on how to utilize effective lessons for traditional (classroom) and distributed (web-based) training environments. It aims to help black community close the existing digital and economic gap, and this program will have worldwide as well as regional impact. This program is intended to accomplish the following goals:

- ✓ Give program participants diversified skills related to sophisticated, high-growth technology and science careers industry workforce skills with objective of replacing more than half of the current workers who are expected to retire in the next five to ten years.
- ✓ Address the misperception that knowledge of science, technology, and mathematics is difficult to acquire, which continues to discourage young black people from taking advantage of these opportunities.
- ✓ Use athletics and sports programs to energize young program participants to be more proficient in math, science, and information technology.
- ✓ Include experienced, about-to-retire workers in the program so they can transfer their knowledge and skills to younger participants.

To satisfy this requirement, we plan to target black, youth-development programs that face a series of practical considerations in deciding whether to expand capacity to meet school- or district-wide service demand, including

- ✓ the impact of expansion on program focus,
- ✓ hiring and training skilled staff to maintain program quality, and
- ✓ how to manage rapid growth without jeopardizing long-term organizational health.

School districts in some parts of the world also face challenges in identifying partners for expanded afterschool programs.

Dissemination

Traditional methods of teaching—presenting instructional materials with a trained instructor—had the advantage of allowing faculty to adjust teaching methods, presentation speed, level of intensity, and format according to class response and feedback. This was key to providing an optimal atmosphere for learning.

A lot of time has been spent on developing one-on-one teacher-pupil relationships, techniques, and methods for improving presentations that require some form of class participation or response. These responses are the measuring stick that traditionally were used to grade instructors. However, with the advent of computer-based lessons, there is no advantage to pupil feedback. The objective is still to optimize the learning atmosphere but without the aid of instructors. At present, there is a gap between learning objectives and the online utilization of instructional materials. BTA has assembled training-development handbooks to guide personnel how to adapt lessons for traditional classroom or web-based delivery. This will allow learning to occur in much friendly environment.

Such utilization decisions will include lesson strategy, specific methods, and interface guidance. We will apply literature in fields such as instructional technology, message design, distance education, and cognitive psychology to analyze the course syllabus. The project will assess if it is feasible to use a web-based atmosphere to teach others. This will be further verified through a comparative analysis using existing literature for the purpose of applying a methodology or algorithm in the applications. The analysis will compare such areas as instructional technology, message design, cognitive psychology, distance learning, distributed training, and reports on experience in lesson utilization. BTA will develop a performance-based assessment system that will provide data regarding program participants' readiness for competitive level high-skill work.

We also plan to build an electronic program-tracking System to provide reliable data on the program outcomes. The findings will be disseminated locally through a series of high-profile community meetings, workshops, briefings, community colleges, and professional organizations. Members of the collaborating organizations will be kept informed through organizational publications. Other modes of dissemination will include regional and national educational conferences, electronic publications, and teleconferences.

We will offer recommendations for designing web-based computer lessons using the above-mentioned approaches, identify research gaps in the literature, and provide guidance in drafting lessons. This guidance will be in a handbook format and include an organizing structure for designing both web- and classroom-based lesson delivery. BTA personnel will be familiar with this guidance, which also will define the research gaps identified above. Apply a computer-based, instructional-design tool to be adopted by government and commercial instructional-material developers as guidance on how to design lessons in the traditional and distributed instructional environments. The outcome of this product will be adopted as the model for web-based learning.

A technology-based learning (TBL) format will transform the way of lessons distributed via all types of electronic technology—including the Internet, intranets, satellite broadcasts, audiotape and videotape, online conferences, chat rooms, bulletin boards, webcasts, and CD-ROMs.

Program Modules
BTA will work closely with the advisory committee to identify which skills will equip black people to compete in science and technology. BTA will seek course designers and content experts from business and academia. They will assemble data on existing distance-learning curricula from a broad range of sources. The project will serve as a clearing house for curricula under construction and provide data on emerging technologies. BTA's staff will work with their project partners to obtain input from the workforce.

Graduates of the program will have the skills that organizations are seeking. Program modules will be reviewed by the advisory board. The modules will be developed with the community's economic development in mind. This can only enhance the program's design and implementation. In order to perform a data-driven analysis, we will interface with industry representatives, construction companies, education, the workforce, labor management organizations, and other worldwide and regional agencies. To satisfy the industry workforce skills requirements, we plan to develop and offer appropriate modules to the program participants.

Course Outline
The program schedule and graduation requirements will be designed to satisfy organizational recommendations:
- ✓ Module 1: Basic IT (I)
- ✓ Module 2: Basic IT (II)
- ✓ Module 3: Soft Skills
- ✓ Module 4: Communication Skills
- ✓ Module 5: Manufacturing Skills

Module 1 (100 Hours): Basic IT (I)
- ✓ How to Use Internet Explorer
- ✓ How to Use Google
- ✓ How to Use Microsoft Outlook
- ✓ How to Use Microsoft Word
- ✓ How to Use Microsoft PowerPoint
- ✓ How to Use Microsoft Excel
- ✓ Homework Assignment

Module 2 (100 Hours): Basic IT (II)
- ✓ How to Use Microsoft XP?
- ✓ How to Use Linux?
- ✓ How to Use Microsoft FrontPage
- ✓ Web Design 101
- ✓ How to Use Photoshop
- ✓ Graphic Design 101
- ✓ How to receive Microsoft Certification
- ✓ How to Use Microsoft Access
- ✓ Homework Assignment

Module 3 (100 Hours) Soft Skills
- ✓ Creative Problem Solving
- ✓ Interpersonal Communication
- ✓ Critical Thinking

✓ Adapting to Technological Change
✓ Client/Server Computing Architecture
✓ Client/Server Computing Application
✓ Homework Assignment

Module 4 (100 Hours): Communication Skills
✓ How to Interface with People of Diverse Educational and Cultural Backgrounds
✓ How to Communicate in Written and Spoken English
✓ How to Manage Time, Prioritize, and Think Strategically
✓ How to Translate Theory into Practice
✓ How to Use Science and Math to Make Decisions
✓ How to Employ Computer-Based Tools
✓ How to Sustain Environmental Development

Modules 5 (100 Hours): Manufacturing Skills
✓ Review of Workshop Material
✓ Business Basics
✓ Thinking Like an Executive
✓ Description of a Business Simulator
✓ Relationship to Workshop Objectives
✓ Homework Assignment

Strategic Importance of Agile Manufacturing
✓ Manufacturing and Strategic Planning
✓ Competing in a Challenging Environment
✓ Integration of Manufacturing into the Enterprise
✓ Changing Paradigms
✓ Manufacturing Approaches, Structures, and Models
✓ Characteristics of Successful Manufacturing Organizations
✓ Integrated Product Teams and Concurrent Engineering/DFM
✓ Reengineering Products and Processes
✓ Information Technology Support in Manufacturing
✓ Cycle Time, Productivity, and Profitability
✓ Keys to Competitive Success

Total Productive Maintenance
- ✓ Introduction to TPM
- ✓ The Basic Concepts
- ✓ Relationships to TQM, JIT, ABM, and TEI
- ✓ Roadmap for TPM Implementation
- ✓ Organization, Planning, Implementation, Assessment
- ✓ Equipment Losses and Calculation of Overall
- ✓ Equipment Effectiveness
- ✓ Workplace Improvement
- ✓ Industry Housekeeping Using 5S

A Note about Funding
This program is too costly and too risky for even a group of companies to fund. Diverse technical resources will be needed to tackle the problem. The answer is to form consortia, as will be shown in following chapter.

Chapter 12

A Strategic Approach

This chapter restates the reasons for the current economic conditions in the black community. Black people are where they are today because of their limited skills and expertise in science- or technology-related subjects, not because they lack the necessary resources. As noted in previous chapters, in terms of natural resources (agricultural, mineral, etc.), Sub-Saharan Africa is the wealthiest continent in the world. Much of this wealth, however, remains untapped, due to the limited scientific and technological skills available to develop these resources into marketable products. This chapter focuses on getting black people the skills and knowledge they need to develop Africa's abundant natural resources.

We have identified the problem and suggested an academic solution. Now, we will consider how to connect the problem to the academic solution. To ensure that black people are united in this effort, we will select universities from each country in Sub-Saharan Africa to collaborate with universities in the United States for the first time. This joint effort will promote unity and teamwork within the black community as its members strive to gain an advantage in the competitive world market.

This program will act as the catalyst for uniting African and African American institutions. True collaborative networks will be possible. Because the program will be a high-risk and long-term venture, it will be challenging to generate the necessary funding. Finding matching funds will minimize individual risk, so that investments can be made for the long term. An important consideration is whether black people alone can successfully fund this program, considering that black athletes and entertainers have been unable to leverage their talents in other areas:

Table 1c, at the beginning of this book, breaks down of the racial composition in American professional sports. Now we will use the same table to demonstrate that black people have missed their opportunity to pursue economic security.

	White %	Black %
Track	20%	80%
Football	12%	88%
Basketball	11%	89%
Baseball	30%	70%
Boxing	10%	90%

Table 12a: The breakdown of white and black athletes in professional sports in the United States.

Based upon the figures in table 12a, black athletes dominate. With 13 percent of the American population, black athletes dominate track and field, with about 80 percent, compared to only 20 percent of white athletes. In football, black players dominate the game with about 88 percent, compared to 12 percent of white players. There are about 89 percent of black basketball players and 11 percent of white players. In baseball, black players dominate the game with about 70 percent, compared to 30 percent of white players. Black boxers dominate the sports; 90 percent of American fighters are black and 10 percent are white.

When these figures are compared to the statistics for science and technology, it is clear that black people are misusing their talents.

Since the middle of the twentieth century, black entertainers have made significant progress in acting, music, dancing, and comedy. Yet, they have not been able to own their own movie production companies or demonstrate any leadership role in this business domain. In professional sports, black participation is dominant, but the same is not true in entertainment. Even with their achievements, for example, black actors still can count on one hand the number of their group who have won the prestigious Oscar.

Black progress in the entertainment and sports industries has created employment opportunities for less than 1 percent of the black population, which is 13 percent of the entire US population. This adds to the 11 percent black unemployment rate.

It is clear that the richest black people in the United States are entertainers and athletes. Therefore, if one wants to raise money for any purpose, he or she must first go this group. We will examine whether this group actually will help fund a high-tech project, such as the one described in this book, will be investigated in a later chapter.

During the eighteenth, nineteenth, and early twentieth centuries, eighteen distinguished black scientists and inventors became involved with science and technology, because they knew the black community could not succeed economically without significant involvement in those fields. These distinguished black scientists and inventors included:

- ✓ Benjamin Banneker, 1731–1806, mathematician
- ✓ Andrew J. Beard, 1849–ca.1921, steam engine specialist
- ✓ George W. Carver, 1860–1943, botanist and agricultural chemist
- ✓ Dr. Charles R. Drew, 1904–1950, medical researcher
- ✓ James Forten Sr., 1766–1842, navigation specialist
- ✓ Lloyd A. Hall, 1894–1971, food chemist
- ✓ Frederick M. Jones, 1892–1961, refrigeration specialist
- ✓ Percy L. Julian, 1899–1931, organic chemist
- ✓ Ernest E. Just, 1883–1941, biologist
- ✓ Lewis H. Latimer, 1848–1928, electrical engineer
- ✓ Joseph Lee, 1849–1905(?), baking technology specialist
- ✓ Jan E. Matzeliger, 1852–1889, shoe machine specialist
- ✓ Elijah J. McCoy, 1843–1929, mechanical engineer
- ✓ Garrett A. Morgan, 1875–1963, traffic signal inventor
- ✓ Norbert Rillieux, 1806–1894, sugar technology specialist
- ✓ Lewis Temple, 1800–1854, whaling technology specialist
- ✓ Granville T. Woods, 1856–1910, electro-mechanical specialist
- ✓ Louis T. Wright, 1891–1952, clinical antibiotic researcher

Black people not only failed to capitalize on these already established scientific and technological foundations, they also failed to explore the use of any Sub-Saharan natural resources., despite powerful evidence that these resources hold strong economic benefits.

To persuade these wealthy black entertainers and athletes to contribute financially to this new technological and scientific crusade, we first must convince them science and technology can deliver enormous economic power to the black community. We will have to show that Sub-Saharan resources can allow a black-owned firm to employ more black employees in a year than both the entertainment and sports industries combined. Furthermore, such an entity could educate African and African American communities on how technology can promote grassroots efforts and improve the general quality of life.

These anticipated economic benefits are based on the potential offered by medium-sized, hi-tech companies. If they can create such impressive economic opportunities, imagine the enormous opportunities that will arise from hi-tech companies the size of Boeing, or Lockheed Martin, or IBM. While employees of black-owned hi-tech companies may rise to the top of the economic ladder, their earnings certainly will take them out of poverty and enable them to help other Blacks as well, thereby establishing greater economic security.

The goal of this book is to ascertain that black people recognize all the opportunities available to them in science and technology and capitalize on those opportunities. If black people can identify themselves with science- and technology-related careers, they will create the momentum they need to accelerate in the twenty-first century with a superior financial status. History has shown that the Native Americans who lived the United States before it was "discovered" by Europeans were unable to satisfy the manual labor requirements of the colonists. This forced Europeans to look for a different group of people to meet their labor requirements. They discovered that black Africans possessed the required skills.

These superior skills present another opportunity for black people; in conjunction with the abundant African resources, those skills should have given the black community economic power. Despite of these superior characteristics, the creditability, integrity, and prestige of black people have been significantly damaged and suppressed by white people. Black people have been told that they are not as bright as other races and should therefore focus all their efforts on specific careers.

This trend does not have to continue. Today, black people must advocate to their youth, by all necessary means, that skills in science, engineering, communication, and manufacturing can help them gain superior economic status. The required skills are listed below.

Science and Technology Goals

1. Strengthen young people's commitment to remain in school and study science, mathematics and engineering, emphasizing that science and engineering are skills for meeting the challenges imposed by the fast-changing business world.
2. Illustrate the importance of science, mathematics, and communication skills in everyday life.
3. Expose youth to a broad range of participatory activities in science, mathematics, and engineering, including research and interactions with engineers and scientists.
4. Offer youth information about and guidance in the career-exploration process, including the academic preparation needed for a variety of professions in science and engineering.
5. Emphasize that science and engineering are sources of hope and economic vitality.
6. Emphasize that science and technology represent alternative approaches to narrowing the wide economic gap between black and white people, which can bring about social unity among all races.

Communication Goals

1. Interface with people of diverse educational and cultural backgrounds.
   - ✓ Recognize that everyone can make a contribution.
   - ✓ Remember that prejudice impedes problem solving and impairs productivity.

2. Communicate in well-written and well-spoken English.
    - ✓ Good ideas must be presented effectively
    - ✓ Individuals must be able to articulate their points of view

3. Manage time, prioritize, and think strategically.
    - ✓ In an empowered work environment, appropriate skills are necessary.

4. Translate theory into practice.
    - ✓ Solving problems requires conceptual knowledge about a specific problem.
    - ✓ Learning how to frame questions and derive solutions is skill developed by practice.

5. Use science and math, including statistics.
    - ✓ To analyze problems and continuously improve productivity, scientific and engineering knowledge is a critical element.

6. Employ computer-based tools.
    - ✓ Automation affects design, production, sales, accounting, and administration.
    - ✓ Small businesses need to know how to use the latest tools to maximize efficiency.

7. Sustain environmental development.
    - ✓ Production planning and design must address the impact of economic, cultural, environmental, and technological factors on the total ecosystem.

Manufacturing Goals

1. Manufacturing
    - ✓ integrated manufacturing
    - ✓ intelligent processing
    - ✓ system-management technologies
    - ✓ product design
    - ✓ product development
    - ✓ manufacturing

2. Materials
   - ✓ materials development linked to performance
   - ✓ synthesis and processing of materials
   - ✓ ability to use a wide group of materials, such as metals and alloys, ceramics, polymers, and composites
   - ✓ exploitation of new materials for electronic, magnetic, and photonic applications
   - ✓ thin film processing

3. Information and Service
   - ✓ software engineering
   - ✓ storage products
   - ✓ display
   - ✓ computer simulation and modeling

4. Integration of Technology
   - ✓ technology transfer
   - ✓ miniaturization of products and device
   - ✓ systems automation
   - ✓ micromechanics
   - ✓ systems control (electromechanical)
   - ✓ multimedia technologies

5. Environment
   - ✓ efficient use of energy and materials
   - ✓ waste minimization
   - ✓ pollution prevention
   - ✓ alternative materials and processes
   - ✓ recovery and recycling
   - ✓ sensors to monitor materials

The progress of black people in entertainment and athletics has not been very significant, because they have not dominated these industries. However, when their progress in this area is compared to their progress in other areas, things look a bit more encouraging. Unfortunately, black people fail to point their young people in the direction of science or technology, which is misleading. Black youth believe black people are only good at sports or entertainment. As a result, these are the careers they pursue. This creates problems, because they are not motivated to pursue careers in science or technology (see table 12a).

We might assume that black entertainers and athletes are not doing much to help the economic status of the black community. Their only goal is individual achievement, as is the case with many other black people. This problem is worsened by the news media. Almost every report about black people is negative. On the television, black people are portrayed only as entertainers; as a result, young black people think those are the only careers to which they can aspire. Consequently, black youngsters ignore careers in science or technology. No black child has ever seen a black engineer or scientist on television. If the problem stopped here, it would not be very damaging. But the problem goes much further.

Chapter 13

A Superior Economic Status

This chapter repeats certain key elements to reinforce the concept that technology is key to economic security and the only logical approach for black people seeking economic power. It is, therefore, worth repeating the key advancements made by black people up to this point:

- ✓ The expulsion of Europeans from Sub-Saharan Africa, which resulted in the independence of many African countries. Dr. Nnamdi Azikiwe led this crusade.
- ✓ The restoration of social equality and justice to the African American. Dr. Martin Luther King Jr. led this crusade.

These two major achievements because in both cases black people performed as a team and fought for a common purpose. Now our challenge is to work together to generate funds to implement this project to achieve economic security in the black community. Considering that various black individuals possess great wealth, in theory raising the money should not be very difficult. However, since it is difficult for black entertainers and athletes to help black people working in other areas, this effort will be difficult and challenge to accomplish. We will develop a methodology to unite black people from both sides of the equation to work together in this effort. We will seek a prominent, influential person with access to black celebrities. This person will work hand in hand with black scientists and technology experts. This joint effort will focus on generating the funds needed to accomplish our goal. The scientists and technology experts will make persuasive presentations. We will make arrangements to get the celebrities together.

I now will explain why this is the time to make the move. We will tell the celebrities about the economic benefits associated with technology development. We will assure them that their investment is wise and will return maximum profits. We will also seek their input on technology development. We will emphasize, over and over, that African resources are most appropriate for this effort and carry the following financial benefits and opportunities:

1. Improved understanding of obscure African natural resources and the objective exploration of their superior qualities, which can be used to develop products for the world market.
2. Identification of American products that can be profitable to African economy once we apply basic engineering fundamentals such as fluid dynamics, stress, aerodynamics; and thermal analysis to determine model deficiencies, design adequacy, proper performance, and performance anomalies. This also will identify opportunities for exporting products to Sub-Saharan Africa.

Chapter 14

A Call to Action

This chapter addresses the need for a program that will give black community access to the following:

- ✓ manufacturing technology
- ✓ education and technology transfer
- ✓ technology transfer and collaboration
- ✓ government roles
- ✓ academia and the government in industrialization
- ✓ total quality management (TQM)

The problems of the black community, particularly in African countries, cannot be addressed until black people are able to join the rest of the world in technological development. Regions that lack a strong industrial base force everyone to clamor for jobs with the government, since it is the only business around. Since the government cannot possibly provide employment for all people, corruption and unhealthy competition for leadership are the result, leading to unstable governments. It is therefore clear that the economic, social, and political progress of black Africa can be advanced by encouraging the creation of local industries that can employ the growing population, provide consumer goods to local markets, export products to other countries, and attract foreign investors.

Many African countries are seeking to move from an agriculture-based to an industry-based economy. To ensure the success, these countries need to develop technical knowhow and the ability to obtain technical data and information, which are abundant in the Western world. Those in the West need to be made aware of the efforts and the capabilities of African manufacturers and to explore methods of cooperation for the benefit of their respective economies. Western scientists, who are at the forefront of industrial research and development efforts, will desire to meet and discuss pertinent issues with African scientists, particularly those who are dealing with problems in manufacturing. Modern techniques will give African scientists ideas about how to tackle problems without reinventing the wheel. American scientists will benefit from the exchange of knowledge as well. A grant from the National Science Foundation, for example, might fund the development of manufacturing technology.

African industries will need to conform to international and local standards in the following ways:

- ✓ develop import substitution
- ✓ establish private-sector funding of industrial research
- ✓ attach research departments to industry
- ✓ deal with politicians' reluctance change from service to manufacturing
- ✓ deal with the lack of government funding
- ✓ determine a new education structure
- ✓ promote the need for a technology-based economic analysis
- ✓ encourage a paradigm shift toward a strong export-based culture
- ✓ develop robust policies to counteract the effect of external forces, such as the International Monetary Fund to help African declining currency
- ✓ train workers in the use of modern technology
- ✓ develop a master plan for industrial and technological development
- ✓ find ways to promote products manufactured in Africa

African industries need to move from rudimentary and traditional manufacturing methods to more advanced methods in order to compete with countries from Southeast Asia for high-tech projects. Obviously, the problems and ideas are many, and thus our aim is to inspire a dialogue among the various sectors.

Conclusion

I believe this is a very important book. In my experience, I have not encountered any books that examine the causes of black poverty from a science and technology perspective. If black people plan to enjoy the economic power of which they have been deprived for hundreds of years, they must change their current strategy, and focus extensively on the approach advocated here. Science and technology will give black people the recognition they very much deserve and give them economic power. I hope this book will make a difference in your life.

References

1. Anand, N. (1978) An integrated approach to research on medicinal plants. Symp. UNIDO Technical Consultation on production of Drugs from Medicinal Plants in Developing Countires, Lucknow, India, 13-20 March, 1978 UNIDO Doc No. ID/WG. 271/3

2. Integrated Approach to Development of New Drugs from Plants and Indigenous Remedies, Nitya Anand & Swarn Nityanand, Central Drug Research Instiute, Lucknow, India 1984

3. Natural Products and Drug Development, Alfred Benzon Symposium 20. Editors: P. Krogsgaard-Larsen, S. Brogger Christensen, H. Kofod, Munksgaard, Copenhagen 1984

4. Structure-Activity Studies and Development of Drugs from Cannabinoids, Raj K. Razdan, Sisa Incorporated, Cambridge, Massachusetts, USA, 1984.

5. Scientific utilization of Native Black African Herbs (NBAH) as cost effective countermeasure against nuclear and space radiation. Raymond Chukwu. Lockheed Missiles & Space Company; Sunnyvale, California, June 1986.

6. Journal of Natural Products, 1996, Vol. 59, No 6.

7. Niruriside, a new HIV REV/RRE Binding Inhibitor from Phyllanthus niruri. Jingfang Qian-Cutrone, Stella Huang, John Trimble, Hui Li, Pin-Fang Lin, Masud Alam, Steve E. Klohr, and Kathleen F. Kadow, October 1995.

8. Five New Anthocyanins, Ternatins A3, B4, B3, B2, and D2, from Clitoria ternatea Flowers. Norihiko Terahara and Masahiro oda, Department of Food Science and Technology, College of Horticulture, Minami-Kyushu University, Takanabe, Miyazaki 884, Japan. Toshiro Matsui and Yutaka Osajima, Department of Food Science and technology, Faculty of Agriculture, Kyushu University, Fukuoka 812, Japan. Norio Saito, Chemical Laboratory, Meiji-gakuin University, Totsuka-ku, Yokohama 224, Japan. Kenjiro Toki, Laboratory of Floriculture, College of Horticulture, Minami-Kyushu University, Takanabe, Miyazaki 884, Japan. Toshio Honda, Institute of Medicinal Chemistry, Hoshi University, Shinagawa-ku, Tokyo 142, Japan. 1995.

9. Isolation of Two New Antinflammatory Biflavanoids from Sarcophyte piriei. Abiodun Ogundaina, Mohamed Farah, Premila Perera, Gunnar Samuelsson, and Lars Bohlin, Division of Pharmacognosy, Biomedical Centre, Uppsala University, Box 579, S-751 23 Uppsala, Sweden, 1995.

10. Blacks and Technology, The Shift of Economic Power to Blacks in the 21st Century, Raymond Chukwu, Duncan & Duncan Inc, Edgewood, MD, May 1998.

11. COUNTERMEASURES FOR THE EFFECTS OF PROLONGED WEIGHTLESSNESS (A86-28776 12-12); p. 655-663 Univelt, Inc. San Diego, CA; 1985

12. Gaffney F.A. 1987, SPACELAB LIFE SCIENCES FLIGHT EXPERIMENTS: An Integrated Approach to the Study of Cardiovascular Deconditioning and Orthostatic Hypotension, Acts Astronautics 15(5), 291-294.

13. Buchanan P. 1987, BONE AND MUSCLE CONSIDERATION OF SPACE FLIGHT HABITATION, Nihon University Symposium on Aerospace Science, Tokyo 5-9, December 1987.

14. Cowin S. (Ed): BONE MECHANICS, CRC Press. Boca Raton, Florida 1989

15. Graff RF: WAVE MOTION IN ELASTIC SOLIDS. Ohio State University Press. Columbus, OH 1975

16. ICRP 1977. THE INTERNATIONAL COMMISSION ON RADIATION PROTECTION, RECOMMENDATION OF THE INTERNATIONAL COMMISSION ON RADIOLOGICAL PROTECTION. ICRP PUBLICATION 26, PERGAMON PRESS. OXFORD, NEW YORK, USA.

17. E.J. Hall and J.S. Bedford, Dose rate: its effect on the survival of HeLa cells irradiated with gamma rays. Radiation Res. 22, 305-315 (1964)

18. Sinclair, W.K. (ED), "RADIATION PROTECTION TODAY,"
    Proceedings of the 25th Annual Meeting of the National Council on Radiation Protection and Measurement, NCRP Proceedings No. 11, NCRP: Bethesda, MD; April 1990.

19. Klein K. E. 1988, BIOMEDICAL RESEARCH AND APPLICATION IN SPACE: Status and Perspectives of European Activities, Interdisciplinary Science Reviews (ISR) (in press).

20. JOURNAL OF GEOPHYSICAL RESEARCH, VOL 86, NO. C12, PAGES, C. RANGARAJAN AND C. D. EAPEN, DEC. 20, 1981

21. U.S. Congress, Office of Technology Assessment, OTA-N-405, 1990, p.225.

22. Developing mineralization agents from Native Black African Herbs and Plants as cost effective alternative medicine against bone demineralization associated with aging; radiation related and prolonged weightlessness. Raymond Chukwu, Bio Chemical Technology Aerospace, 1988.

23. Natural Products and Drug Development, Central Drug Research Institute, Lucknow, 226001, India, 1984

24. Moussoukhoye Diop, Abdoulaye Samb, Valera Costantino, and Alfonso Mangon; Department de Chimie, Faculte des Sciences et Techniques, Universite Cheikh Anta Diop, Dakar, Senegal and dipartimento di Chimica delle Sostanze Naturali, Universita degli Studi di Napoli "Federico II" Via D. Montesano 49, 80131 Napli, Italy, 1992.

25. Jingfang Qian-Cutrone, Stella Huang, John Trimble, Hui Li, Pin-Fang Lin, Masud Alam, Steve E. Klohr, and Kathleen F. Kadow; Bristol-Myers Squibb Pharaceuticals Research Institute, 5 Research Parkway, Wallingford, Connecticut 06492.

26. FIELD OF FOOD IRRADIATION; National Technical Information Services; SPRINGFIELD, VA; 1980;

27. Markham, K.R. Geiger, H; Jaggy, H. Phytochemistry 1992, 31. 1009-1011.

28. THE EFFECTS Q ON SHORT PERIOD P WAVES FROM EXPLOSIONS IN CENTRAL ASIA: THOMAS C. BACHE; SCIENCE APPLICATIONS, INC., LA JOLLA, CA APRIL 1984

29. World Health Issue, June 1983

30. Nationa Institute of Health, SBIR Review Committee, Maryland, 1999

31. National Institute of Health, SBIR/STTR Review Committee, Marylad, 1994

32. United States Housing and Household, Economic Statistics Division, Department of Commerce, Washington DC 1996

33. (Giambarresi, L. and Jacobs, A.J., Radioprotectants, Chap. 14. In: Military Radiobiology. Eds, Conklin, J.J., Walker, R.I. Academic Press: Orlando; 1987).

34. African American Health Facts (The Office of Minority Health Resource Center, Washington, DC 1997.

35. National Center for Health Statistics, Advance Report of Final Mortality Statistics, Monthly Vital Statistics Report, Vol. 45 No. 3(S), September 30, 1996.

36. African American HIV/AIDS, A Guide to Selected Resources, CDC National AIDS Clearinghouse, June 1997.

37. Education Focus for Improvement, Silicon Valley's Path to Survival in a Competitive World, Initiated by the Applied Technology Institute, San Jose University, July 1992

38. California Employment Training Panel, Special Employment and Education, Planning and Research Unit, Sacramento, CA, November 1, 1994.

39. Manufacturing Education and Training, National Science Foundation, Arlington, Virginia 1995

About Black Technologies Advancement

Located in Santa Clara County, part of Silicon Valley, Black Technologies Advancement (BTA) was established in 1992 as a 501(c)3 nonprofit research and educational institute to promote scientific research and technology development. Its goal is to answer the question, *is technology against black people, or are black people against technology?* Either way, black people must identify with science- or technology-related products before they can overcome the frustrating and shameful poverty that faces a large percentage of their community. Black poverty can be attributed to the fact that black people are not associated with any science- or technology-related products, without which every race will experience difficult economic growth. BTA is committed to changing this equation by developing the following services:

- ✓ free scholarship information for students
- ✓ free job training
- ✓ free grant-writing workshops
- ✓ HIV/AIDS research program
- ✓ renewable energy research and development
- ✓ aerospace research

Scholarship Information Program
Given the difficulties that low-income students experience with financing their education, BTA acts as an ambassador between them and granting-making organizations. The goal is to create an opportunity for students to attend schools of their choice.

Mission
Given that there is relatively little information to demonstrate whether treatments incorporating African herbs are safe or beneficial, BTA is dedicated to generating such data and assessing their impact on the black economy. It will do this by creating opportunities for black people to participate in the competitive and fast-changing technological environment. In this capacity, BTA has created scholarship programs (listed below) for low-income students in Sub-Saharan Africa and

the United States, with the aim of developing a workforce that can promote Africa's natural resources on the world market. BTA expects these resources to dominate the global economy in the not too distant future.

BTA's scholarships will target the following:

- ✓ African undergraduate students transferring to American community colleges
- ✓ Undergraduate and graduate students studying at American universities
- ✓ American high school students who desire to complete their education in (preferably) English-speaking Sub-Saharan countries; this will give them superior academic preparation for their university coursework when they return to the United States
- ✓ African undergraduate students who want to receive an American education and then return to their home countries to utilize that education
- ✓ African and American graduate students who seek to acquire their education in a specific area and return either to the United States or their African nations, where they will contribute to the economic expansion of both regions

Program Justification

Despite decades of effort, Sub-Saharan Africa remains impoverished. The region is poorer today than it was in 1960, in some cases by very wide margins. As a result, Sub-Saharan Africa has been the site of large-scale experiments to reform its economy. However, these ambitious projects have failed to generate sustained economic growth. Sub-Saharan Africa, with its abundant natural resources, is considered the most prosperous region in the world economy, yet its citizens are starved and malnourished. Put differently, the sheer magnitude of this problem, which is overwhelming, calls for an innovative approach to reform the current economic system and education to accommodate African and US business interests. BTA believes that African natural resources can help build a stronger social and economic relationship between Sub-Saharan Africa and the United States. We expect our scholarship program to improve the business relationship between the two regions through the exchange of both information by university graduates who were sponsored by the scholarship program.

Job Training Program

BTA acts as an ambassador between high school dropouts and community-based businesses and service providers. Our goal is to equip this low-income group with occupational skills that will allow organizations to expand.

Program Justification

High school dropouts and professionals in the process of changing jobs will be targeted for this program. Innovations are changing Silicon Valley at unimaginable speeds. However, with only about 53 percent of Silicon Valley youth participating in any postsecondary education or training, and as many as 40 percent dropping out of high school, this progress of this innovation might be at risk. Without technical knowledge, relevant experience, and the skills needed to succeed in the twenty-first-century global economy, the vast majority of these high school dropouts will be destined for low-paying jobs. This could compromise our productivity, undermine our competitiveness in the global marketplace, and place us years behind our international competitors. BTA offers training programs that teach the following skills: technical knowledge, relevant experience, and applied skills. Our job-training program will equip high-school dropouts with confidence, self-esteem, courage, and inner strength as well as the occupational skills to compete in the twenty-first-century economy. This is necessary to create a stronger economy and pro-business environment, which will include the following:

- ✓ the expansion of existing businesses
- ✓ affordable housing for working families
- ✓ employment opportunities
- ✓ wage and salary increases
- ✓ improved job skills

Grant-Writing Workshop

Many individuals and companies—disadvantaged and small businesses, women-owned businesses, and others—are unable to do the following things due to limited resources and lack of skills among their employees:

- ✓ expand an existing business
- ✓ start a new business
- ✓ take innovative products into the marketplace
- ✓ develop new technologies
- ✓ advance scientific knowledge
- ✓ create new technological concepts

The goal of this program is to give businesses and services providers the tools, materials, and resources they need to expand their operations.

Only about 53 percent of small businesses in Silicon Valley participate in any federal grant program, and as many as 40 percent lack the necessary capabilities to prepare and submit a competitive grant application, particularly at a time when the federal government only accepts applications through its Grants.gov system. Without the skills they need to compete in the twenty-first-century global economy, the vast majority of these small businesses—particularly those associated with defense undertakings—are destined for uncertain business futures. That could compromise our productivity, undermine our competitiveness in the global marketplace, and places us years behind our international competitors. We need to equip these businesses with the skills and resources they need to submit their applications through the Grants.gov system. Such skills and resources include the following:

- ✓ how to obtain a DUNS number
- ✓ how to register with the System for Award Management (SAM) at www.sam.gov.
- ✓ how to register on Grants.gov
- ✓ how to search for grant opportunities
- ✓ how to download grant applications
- ✓ how to complete the grant applications
- ✓ how to prepare the application/proposal

Competitive business strategies and training programs will enable these businesses to market their products around the world. BTA has teamed up with Bio Chemical Technology Aerospace in San Jose and the Silicon Valley Training Institute in Sunnyvale to develop such a comprehensive program.

HIV/AIDS Research

The literature of every ancient culture contains accounts of herbs with special healing powers. Traditional systems of Asian medicine, particularly Chinese remedies, have gained worldwide attention. Yet, Sub-Saharan African traditional remedies are neither recognized nor endorsed. As a result, limited scientific data are available to demonstrate whether a particular remedy made from African herbs is safe, beneficial, or leads to a positive outcome, such as

- ✓ reducing the size of a tumor,
- ✓ prolonging or improving quality of life,
- ✓ reducing or eliminating adverse symptoms of toxic treatments, or
- ✓ acting as a countermeasure against HIV/AIDS.

An HIV/AIDS Cure Using Sub-Saharan Herbs

To generate scientific data that will demonstrate that African herbs can be effective countermeasures against diseases, including HIV/AIDS, BTA assembled a group of partners to develop a priori computational methods. Our proposed methods will utilize various categories of African herbs to formulate mathematical equations. The equations can be reconfigured by simplified finite element technique and represented by a finite set of ordinary differential equations with dimensions involving hundreds or even thousands of terms defining the degree of freedom of the herbs and their derivatives. Such a large matrix usually consumes large amounts of costly computer time. We propose to employ, therefore, a balanced realization technique or route approximation method to reduce the size of the matrix into computable finite set of ordinary differential equations. The solution of these equations will exhibit combinations with promising countermeasures against HIV/AIDS and other diseases.

A Web-Based Intervention and Prevention System

With the escalating rate of HIV/AIDS in Sub-Saharan Africa, we need to control the widespread of the deadly disease. More than four hundred organizations are currently participating in the fight. Given that sex is considered to be much of a bedroom affair, even among the adults, African culture does not permit open discussion about sex. Hence, no one would ever dare to discuss anything sex-related with children, including high school students.

Yet HIV/AIDS is 90 percent about sex, nothing else. Despite the large number of organizations in the fight, the number of HIV/AIDS victims and people who are at risk continue to increase at an alarming rate. The magnitude of the problem suggests it is imperative to design different and innovative strategies.

We performed an extensive study on the HIV/AIDS-related methodologies employed by the leading web-based establishments and commercially available products. We discussed our findings with health care professionals and in medical publications to determine user needs. Based upon the research work and the discussions, we determined that these network systems suffer from scientific and technological limitations, which compromise their intended use, particularly in Sub-Saharan nations. We propose to develop an HIV/AIDS intervention and prevention system that can inform high school and college students in rural and urban Africa how to stop the spread of the deadly disease through behavior changes, product distribution/sales, stronger private sector services, collaboration with partners involved with similar research efforts.

Renewable Energy Research and Development

BTA is dedicated to using technology to achieve greater energy efficiency, a more diversified energy portfolio, and a scenario in which renewable energy will provide a high percentage of US electricity.

Project Objectives

Energy prices, supply uncertainties, and environmental concerns are driving the United States to rethink its energy mix and develop diverse sources of clean, renewable energy. As a result, the nation is working toward generating more energy from domestic resources that can be cost-effective and replaced or "renewed" without contributing to climate change or creating an adverse impact on the environment. There is growing consensus within the renewable energy industry that the current approaches will not be able to meet the needs of the United States. The wind energy industry estimates electricity demand will grow by 39 percent between 2005 and 2030, reaching 5.8 billion megawatt-hours by 2030. Renewable energy is expected to play a major role. BTA plans to be an integral part of this effort through advances in computation, networking, and grid monitoring, which have shed light on potential ways to deliver electricity more efficiently and reliably. BTA's renewable-energy research and development projects include

- ✓ using electromagnetic radiation in the form of a laser beam to charge electric vehicles wirelessly,
- ✓ smart wind utility grid (SWUG) knowledge-based expert system for electric vehicle charging stations,
- ✓ offshore wind turbine system integrated diagnostics expert systems,
- ✓ motor program generator for wind turbine composite light weight blade design, and
- ✓ technician's assistant expert systems for wind turbine systems maintenance.

Proposals on each of these items are available for review by potential investors.

BTA's Project to Wirelessly Charge Electric Vehicles

Objectives
BTA is developing the technology that will send electromagnetic radiation via a laser beam to charge electric vehicles wirelessly. A specific goal is to demonstrate continuous (24/7) electric-power transfer from network of laser stations in a way that is greater than anything that has been done before. This milestone appears achievable in a three- to five-year timeframe, perhaps even earlier than that. This proposal is focused on the identification of key technology issues in the real world, setting the stage for commercial electromagnetic

radiation in the form of laser power beaming phenomenon to wirelessly provide electricity on demand where and when needed to recharge or charge electric vehicles. Continuous power from the laser stations is critical because energy storage is the cost that limits market penetration of electric vehicles. This is a high priority in a world where energy prices, supply uncertainties, and environmental concerns are driving people to rethink their energy mix and develop diverse sources of clean, renewable energy. BTA will assemble a multidisciplinary team to meet the project objectives.

Project Description
The public adoption of electric vehicles can benefit the economy. Currently, however, recharging a vehicle requires the driver to physically connect to a charging device. Wireless-charging technology has the potential to significantly increase acceptance and convenience of electric cars and encourage many wary drivers to buy one.

A team at Stanford has designed a highly efficient charging system, which uses magnetic fields to transmit large electric currents that wirelessly charge cars and trucks as they cruise down an all-electric highway. However, this project may not be economically feasible given the cost to revamp the entire highway system with the magnetic fields. In addition, roadbed transmitters and other metals in the pavement might compromise efficiency. We plan to find a faster, cheaper, simpler, more accurate, and more flexible design than the one Stanford has proposed. We will develop, test, refine, and demonstrate the capabilities of electromagnetic radiation in the form of a laser beam. With electromagnetic radiation closer to visible region of spectrum power can be transmitted by converting electricity into a laser beam that is then pointed at a solar cell receiver.

This mechanism is known as "power beaming," because the power is sent to a receiver that can convert it to usable electrical energy. When a laser beam is centered on its panel of photovoltaic cells, for example, a lightweight model plane can fly. We must ensure that the proposed technology will utilize a wide variety of artificial intelligence (AI).

This project will address the following specific objectives: driving range, wireless charging, wireless future.

Driving Range

A wireless charging system would address a major drawback of plug-in electric cars and their limited driving ranges. Most electric vehicles get less than one hundred miles on a single charge, and the battery takes several hours to fully recharge. A charge-as-you-drive system would overcome these limitations. What makes this concept very exciting is that you could potentially drive for an unlimited amount of time. You could actually have more energy stored in your battery at the end of your trip than at the beginning. Laser beams will wirelessly transfer energy (heat or electricity) from one location to another. It is the same basic concept as solar power, where the sun shines on a photovoltaic cell that converts the sunlight to energy. Here, a photovoltaic cell converts laser light to energy. The key differences are that laser light is much more intense than sunlight, it can be aimed at any desired location, and it can deliver power twenty-four hours per day. Power can be transmitted through air or space, or through optical fibers, which is how communications signals are sent today, and it potentially can be sent as far away as the moon.

Wireless Charging

Although it is still largely in the research-and-development stage, wireless power has many potential uses in the real world. Such uses include powering air, ground, and underwater vehicles; replacing electric power wiring and transmission lines in difficult places; and even launching rockets into orbit. In October 2010, Laser Motive further demonstrated how wireless technology can power a quadrocopter in flight. Using a battery that typically would have enabled roughly five minutes of flight, the vehicle flew for nearly twelve and a half continuous hours, powered wirelessly by laser from the ground. This was 150 times the normal battery life. The flight set the following records:

- ✓ It was the longest, hovering flight duration for an untethered electric vehicle. The flight length was limited only by the venue; the quadrocopter and the Laser Motive power system were both capable of continuing indefinitely.

✓ It set the endurance record for any VTOL aircraft in this weight class.

✓ It was the longest beamed-energy-powered flight of any type.

In addition, the flight marked the following key milestones regarding operational laser-powered UAVs:

✓ repeated fully automatic acquisition of UAV by a laser-tracking system

✓ in-flight battery recharging

✓ automatic position hold-in beam, with the laser-tracking system controlling the UAV position

Smart Wind Utility Grid (SWUG) for Plug-In Hybrid Electric Vehicle Charging Stations

For electric vehicles to become a commonplace and a viable replacement for cars with internal combustion engines, millions of city parking spaces will have to be upgraded to allow for convenient, economic charging. One challenge is that the consumption of electricity might compromise other uses of power. We recommend exploring wind energy as a source of power for electric vehicle charging stations.

However, the application of major technologies to store electricity when it is not needed or deliver this stored electricity when demand is high or renewable output is low continued to compromise the solution to the problem of variable wind output. Electric vehicles could address this energy storage problem.

To achieve this objective we propose to utilize knowledge representation and reasoning architecture—based on an automated reasoning tool and the mechanics that govern the load-control dynamics that are already in place for water heaters and air conditioners—to develop and deploy wind energy as a competitive utility grid. This methodology involves a hypothetical reasoning process that is applied to a planning domain that changes over time such as load-control dynamics. This interpretation necessitates the development of hypothetical and temporal reasoning capabilities to provide guidance regarding procedures for addressing identified technology issues.

From these issues, the potential for load-control systems will be reassessed and guidelines developed. This will lead to a plan for the utilization of wind as an energy source for electric cars

Offshore Wind Turbine Systems

An offshore wind turbine system is unavoidable, given that the power extraction equipment must be far from the ground. The deployment in hydrodynamic environment at a shallow (about 0–30 m) below sea level makes this the core technological component in accelerating responsible commercial offshore wind development and deployment.

The proposed system is a powerful tool for achieving US Department of Energy targets of 54 gigawatts (GW) of deployed wind at a cost of 4 cents per kilowatt-hour (kWh) with an interim target of 10 GW of capacity deployed by 2020 at a cost of energy of 5 cents per kWh. This will play a major role in getting wind to provide 20 percent of the electricity in the United States. Therefore the innovation in offshore wind turbine technology hinges on the ability to rely on experts who are capable of responding to changes in wind dynamics and wind turbine systems in the quickest manner possible. This process will isolate and diagnose faults and collect enough data to allow technicians to fix the problem. We will employ trajectory learning and retrieval of parallel processing neural network model of a motor program generator (MPG) for pursuit eye movements and diagnostic systems to simulate wind turbine sensors before we develop our proposed system.

We envision that the proposed system will be highly automated, capable of performing real-time diagnostics, detecting faults, and rapidly isolating the cause of the failure. This will help technicians analyze performance of the offshore wind turbine systems and subsystems. This system will provide an ideal vehicle for developing, demonstrating, and evaluating machine intelligence technologies as well as subsystem diagnostics and maintenance and repair problems.

Motor Program Generator for Wind Turbines: Composite Light-Weight Blade Design

Defects are often introduced during the design of the wind turbine blades, whose composite structures contain variations in fiber content and alignment. This also include none incorporation of intelligent capabilities. To structurally and aerodynamically evaluate composite structures to meet design challenges necessitates innovations to achieve competitiveness in the blade design. One method to address this challenge is to analyze wind turbine power output, which is controlled by rotating the blades around their long axis to change the angle of attack with respect to the relative wind as the blades spin around the rotor hub to determine that high-strength, light-weight, structurally efficient, damage-tolerant, and cost-effective composite materials will meet this design objective.

Meeting such design objective hinges on a multidisciplinary approach that involves a composite system design assistant (CSAD) rule-based expert system, parallel processing neural network model of a motor program generator (MPG) for pursuit eye movements (PEM), and the development of a light-weight composite blade suitable for a wind-driven horizontal axis propeller device capable of delivering significantly more energy than is currently possible. US electricity demand estimated to grow by 39 percent between 2005 and 2030, reaching 5.8 billion megawatt-hours (MWh) by 2030, of which wind is expected to provide 20 percent. Our blade not only will significantly increase energy output, it also will create a more than $10 billion market opportunity by 2015, targeting these four market segments:

- ✓ utility-scale wind power plants, both land-based and offshore
- ✓ community-owned projects, which often produce power for local consumption and sell bulk power under contracts
- ✓ institutional and business applications
- ✓ off-grid home installations and behind-the-meter farm, ranch, and home systems

Technician's Assistant Expert Systems for Wind Turbine Maintenance

To determine the current state of this technology and quantify the threat characteristics given different scenarios of wind turbine complex aerodynamic environment, we conducted a pilot study. We determined that most wind turbine simulators use analog circuitry to compute the complex dynamic response of wind turbines in real time. Our analytical assessment suggests that this will certainly compromise decision-making and the ability to tracking deficiencies and malfunctions in real-time. As a result technicians and operators often criticize these systems for failing to diagnose or isolate faults or to provide enough data to allow them to conduct adequate diagnostics.

The system status (SS) monitoring system is a subsystem of the neural network of the MPG. It will bring wind turbine simulation and analytical systems up to the level of current digital computer systems. This will equip the system with signal processing, pattern recognition, and neural network algorithms to accurately track deficiencies and malfunctions. We focused on developing an autonomous monitoring system capable of real-time diagnostics, fault detection, and resource management and maintenance to ensure that the system can perform the following important tasks on multiple units of wind power plants:

- ✓ real-time fault detection and model validation
- ✓ real-time performance prediction
- ✓ real-time reconfiguration, resource management, and feedback maintenance

We envisioned the proposed system to be highly automated, capable of performing real-time diagnostics and fault detection, and rapidly isolating causes of failure. This will aid technicians with little or no experience with wind turbines.

Aerospace Research and Development
Aerospace research and development is grouped under the following categories:

- ✓ on-board integrated diagnostic motor program generator for commercial aircraft
- ✓ open-architecture, web-enabled system engineering environmental tool

On-Board Integrated Diagnostic Motor Program Generator for Commercial Aircraft

Flight environment challenges often surpass the human ability to respond effectively in real time using today's available technologies. To achieve flight objectives, a pilot must be able to maintain total control of his or her aircraft, while responding to emergencies or changes in aircraft systems in the quickest possible manner, to eliminate mistakes and errors. To assist pilots without reducing their concentration, we will employ trajectory learning and retrieval of the parallel processing neural network model of MPG for pursuit eye movements and diagnostic expert systems to comprehensively model and simulate aircraft sensors. ours will be a highly automated system, capable of performing real-time diagnostics, fault detection, and rapid isolation of problems to equip the pilot with the ability to maintain total control of the aircraft and respond to emergencies or changes as soon as possible manner. The planning for this project is extremely complex and involves numerous experts in various areas of aircraft operations.

Project Description

Increasing demand for expert systems on commercial aircraft requires the identification of computer-processing, remote-data communication and mass memory storage technologies to verify critical aspects of the defined concepts and develop a system specification, implementation approach, and demonstration plan to achieve the design objectives.

The need for an on-board integrated diagnostic motor program generator for commercial aircraft is indicated by serious deficiencies in the current on-board diagnostic system for cockpit instrumentation. This is primarily the selection of the content, format, and modality of information passed to the pilot, which is used to manage the display and control resources in the cockpit. It gives pilots the necessary tools to operate in an environment flooded with massive amounts of data obtained from multiple sources. This is the first in a series of knowledge bases we will develop to evaluate systems and networks in cockpit instruments. Most user interface is accomplished via a combination of an automated reasoning tool and Lisp code. We will determine which technologies, algorithms, and computational methods can help pilots manage their workloads, detect errors, and implement instructions.

Through modeling and simulating sensor data for analysis, development, and benchmarking of decision-making tools and information integration algorithms, we plan to accomplish this mission, which should include accurate modeling of applicable uncertainties associated with the collection and processing of the information passed to the pilot. We will use the following computing techniques: scrip application for intent interfacing and error detection/classification, production rules for display resources management and conflict resolution, and algorithmic models. Expert systems technology is ideally suited for the design, development, diagnosis, and maintenance of aircraft systems and subsystems. Therefore the proposed project hinges on the ability to integrate experts who can respond to changes in aircraft systems in the quickest possible manner and reason intelligently about the aircraft systems.

Open-Architecture, Web-Enabled System Engineering Environmental Tool
This project will analyze soil moisture profiles and land biophysical parameters against compost from recyclables to engineer land fertilization on crops cultivation mechanics. This effort is expected to offer the following advantages to rural commercial and recycling establishments to help farmers maximize their cultivation activities:

- ✓ improve efficiency on waste-collection and waste-management processes
- ✓ improve waste management access to recycling facilities and centers
- ✓ develop methods for profitable utilization of compost
- ✓ utilize composts to engineer robust soil mechanics
- ✓ employ the engineered soil mechanics for healthy cultivation of crops

Project Description
A growing number of Americans suffer from at least one of five chronic conditions: heart disease, cancer, diabetes, hypertension, and chronic obstructive disease (and other serious diseases due to

obesity-related health problems associated with poor diet). The cost of such treatment runs to several hundred million dollars a year. This is further compounded by the growing consensus within the farming industry that current approaches will not allow American farmers to compete in the global marketplace.

There is a need for new technologies to reinvigorate existing farming methodologies while supporting the growth and development of clean recycling technologies. Using remote-sensing technology for more accurate and timely inventories of agricultural resources is one way to address this problem. However, one such effort failed to achieve the growth of organic healthy food at affordable costs to consumers, because the technologies and techniques that were employed dated back to the 1970s. Although the technologies might have been refined since then, the development techniques remains complex and time consuming. BTA plans to pursue entirely new method to achieve faster, cheaper, simpler, more accurate, and more flexible techniques. We want to employ artificial intelligence components to simulate an open-architecture, web-enabled system engineering environmental management tool with the following components:

- ✓ parallel processing neural network model of a motor program generator (MPG) for pursuit eye movements (PEM)
- ✓ expert system technology
- ✓ an automated reasoning tool (ART)
- ✓ on-board automated expert advisors
- ✓ spacecraft- or satellite-acquired land information database
- ✓ compost database
- ✓ computer system with a sophisticated artificial intelligent network system
- ✓ using computer analysis to fertilize soil

This project will employ knowledge representation and reasoning architecture that will be based on the automated reasoning tool. The methodology will involve a hypothetical reasoning process that is applied to a planning domain that changes over time. The interpretation necessitates the development of hypothetical and temporal reasoning capabilities. Such capabilities will be based upon the current and emerging multicenter, low/medium altitude aircraft or sensor mission scheduling system data and land-acquired data phenomena. This includes comparing satellite-acquired, remotely sensed information regarding soil moisture profiles, land biophysical parameters, and compost to intelligently fertilize the land and the crops. This will not only provide healthy food products to consumers; it will also provide key economic advantages to rural commercial and recycling establishments.

www.ingramcontent.com/pod-product-compliance
Lightning Source LLC
Chambersburg PA
CBHW020538290526
45786CB00002B/934